What the media is saying about David M. Voth and The 10 Secrets ...

David Voth's tax secrets, for the taxed-to-death, are a way for people to get even.
Joanne Paulson - The Star Phoenix

Easy-to-read, no-nonsense, tax-avoidance book... Canadians are fed up with Ottawa dining out on their hard-earned pay cheques.
Westwatch - Western Report

Voth's Secrets range from the commonplace to the exotic, adding a little spice to his advice.
Jim Knisley - Leader Post

Easy to read strategies to cut your tax bill. Voth clearly outlines many tax cutting strategies you can put to use immediately.
The Western Canadian

Legitimate tax escapes that many of us might overlook.
Martin Levin - The Globe & Mail

This little book might keep you from ending up poor. Anyone who buys and reads this book... is likely to end up doing things that will more than repay the price it costs.
John Robson - Western Report

Everything in the book is perfectly legal.
Doug Lett – CTV News

Volume Orders

For volume orders of **The 10 Secrets Revenue Canada Doesn't Want You To Know!**, Liberty House Publishing grants a discount on the purchase of **10 or more** copies. For further details contact: Marketing Department, Liberty House Publishing
Fax: (306) 934-0484   Phone: (306) 955-3838
E-mail: **libertyhouse@shaw.ca**

The 10 Secrets Revenue Canada Doesn't Want You To Know!

Written By:

David M. Voth

First published in 1996
Revised & Expanded Edition – Published in 2002
Third printing – April 2004

Published by Liberty House Publishing

Voth, David M., 1958-
The 10 Secrets Revenue Canada Doesn't Want
You To Know!

ISBN 0-9731307-0-9

1.Finance, Personal – Canada.
2. Tax Planning – Canada. I. Title

Although the author has exhaustively researched all sources
to ensure accuracy and completeness of information
contained in this book, the author and publisher assume no
responsibility for errors, inaccuracies, omissions or any
inconsistency herein. Readers should use their own judgment
and/or consult professional advisors for specific applications to
their individual situation.

Scripture quotations are taken from the Holy Bible, New
Living Translation, copyright © 1996. Used by permission of
Tyndale House Publishers, Inc., Wheaton, Illinois 60189.
All rights reserved.

Printed in Canada

Acknowledgements

Jason M. Cloth, CFP
Research Data

John Muzika, B.A., B.Comm., P.Ag., CFP, CLU, Ch.F.C.
Review and Critique

Dwayne Daku
Editing and Inspiration

Malcolm (Mac) Thorpe
Design, Layout and Illustrations

Lesley
Unconditional Love, Acceptance and Encouragement

Table of Contents

David vs. Goliath

Introduction

Taxes in Canada, as you're about to find out if you don't already know, are incredibly high. The percentage of tax that Canadians pay is completely outrageous. While some taxes appear to be reduced, others are increased and new ones added, to continually increase revenues for our politicians to squander. It's the government's version of the shell game!

The average Canadian now pays half of their income in some form of tax, while the highest income earners pay as much as 75% of their income in some form of tax. That's why serious tax planning is more necessary now than ever. Not just for a few of the top income earners but for every Canadian. You owe it to yourself and your family to keep more of what you earn. That is the purpose of this book; to give you more control of what is rightfully yours.

Most books on tax are very complicated, written by accountants for tax planning professionals. Of necessity, due to the complexity of tax laws, they are detailed analytical tomes that are generally boring to read and hard to understand. *The 10 Secrets Revenue Canada Doesn't Want You To Know!*, was written for the average person. Anyone who has a basic understanding of the English language can read and understand the strategies laid out in this book. With this goal in mind, while editing the first edition of this book, I had a high school student read it and tell me if there were any things in it that she could not understand. I edited it until it was understandable by a high school student.

For this reason, professional tax planners have from time to time been critical of the book's simplicity and lack of detail. Well, it wasn't written for them. They already have huge boring tax books on their shelves. This book was written for people who might never read a book on tax and discover some ideas to get back more of what is rightfully theirs. Then, with the help of a financial planner you can implement strategies to get Revenue Canada's hand out of your pockets. *"A mind once stretched by a new idea, never regains its original dimensions"* —Oliver Wendell Holmes.

Furthermore, most books on tax are written to benefit readers in completing their tax returns and are therefore useful only during preparation and submitting returns. **The 10 Secrets Revenue Canada Doesn't Want You To Know!,** was written with planning strategies in mind and therefore is useful throughout the year.

It should be noted that the government agency previously known as Revenue Canada is now called Canada Customs and Revenue Agency (CCRA). The Government of Canada created the new agency through a piece of legislation called Bill C-43. The Bill received royal assent on April 29, 1999 and then subsequent to that, the name was officially changed November 1, 1999.

At the time I wrote the first edition of this book they were called Revenue Canada. I believe that most Canadians still think of them as Revenue Canada, therefore I have not changed the title of the book, nor references within the book, to reflect the new name. Besides, just because a thief changes his clothes, address, or name doesn't make him an honest man of integrity, does it?

Whoever desires liberty should understand these vital facts:

1. *That every man who puts money in the hands of a "government" (so called), puts into its hands a sword which will be used against himself to extort more money from him, and also to keep him in subjection to its arbitrary will.*

2. *That those who will take his money, without his consent, in the first place, will use it for his further robbery and enslavement, if he presumes to resist their demands in the future.*

—Lysander Spooner, author No Treason (1808-1887)

Section 1
–The Problem–

⪰ Chapter 1 ⪯
Legacy Of Debt

Christmas is a time when kids tell Santa what they want and adults pay for it. Deficits are when adults tell the government what they want and their kids pay for it.
—Richard Lamm

Let me ask you a question:

Have You Ever Felt More Aggravated With Our Government?

Try to remember a time in your life when all levels of government were more messed up than they are today. It is very sad how poorly the Federal, Provincial and Local leaders are running the financial affairs of our country.

You cannot pick up a paper, magazine or watch TV, without seeing another story about government debt, budget deficits, cuts in services, and government infighting. We watch on as our governments fund programs that you would not be willing to fund in a free market. For example: In 1995, the government claimed the firearm registration program would cost $85 million over 5 years. The costs are now at $700 million and rising. What does this program promise? *"This year will go down in history. For the first time, a civilized nation has full gun registration. Our streets will be safer, our police more efficient, and the world will follow our lead into the future!"* —Adolph Hitler, in a 1933 speech. Remember, *"Those who do not learn from the mistakes of history are doomed to repeat them."* —George Santayana.

Canadians are seriously concerned about their government's handling of public money and have lost faith in their politicians. Our governments are living beyond their means and borrow dangerously to do so.

The statistics on Canada's debt paint a dismal picture. The idea that Canadians owe $600 billion (the approximate federal debt) ignores federal obligations and indirect debt, as well as all the liabilities of the provincial and local governments.

The Fraser Institute, Canada's leading economic think tank, reports that by the end of 1999, Canada's total all-government gross debt was equal to $3.5 trillion. This is equal to 410% of Canada's gross domestic product (GDP - all the goods and services produced in Canada in one year) or over 10 times all of our annual exports.

Expressed more personally, the Canadian government owes $115,772 for every Canadian citizen or $243,632 for each taxpayer. These statistics show that Canadian governments have accumulated an unsustainable level of debt. Even if governments took 100% of every dollar of income generated, it would take over four years to pay back the debt and fully fund all programs.

And, this debt is worsening by $100+ billion per year. On March 31, 1995 the total debt was "ONLY" $3.1 trillion dollars, $104,919 for every Canadian citizen. This makes Canada:

The World's 5th Most Severely Indebted Nation!

This overwhelming debt caries with it a huge interest cost. In 1997/1998, Canadian governments spent almost $74 billion on interest payments; that is, 8.7 percent of GDP and 21.6 percent of exports. Since there are now over 30 million people in this country, the annual interest payments on the debt is equal to $2,500 per person per year.

The interest charges alone, on Canada's federal public debt, eats up more than ⅓ of Ottawa's total annual revenue!

What would happen to you or your family if ⅓ of your annual income went to pay the interest on your debts? One thing is for sure, you'd be declaring bankruptcy or seeking some serious debt relief.

Another major concern is the currency risk associated with that portion of the debt that is owed to foreign governments and institutions. A significant portion of the debt of many provinces is held in foreign currency. The necessity to pay interest on, and ultimately repay the debt in foreign currencies creates an additional risk for all of us. Deterioration in the value of the Canadian dollar increases the cost of paying the debt in foreign currency.

Why am I talking to you about government debt? Is this book supposed to be about politics or how we can change things in government? I wish. Really, my purpose is to illustrate how these government money problems affect all of us. And, most importantly — What, if anything, can we do to protect **ourselves?**

So, how does the government's poor handling of our money affect us?

It affects us in many ways — through interest rates, devaluing our dollar, etc. But, the biggest effect is the result of the government's erroneous idea that to pay the interest on the debt and to continue to keep spending, they must tax us! Each year at budget time the nation holds it's collective breath and waits as the various levels of government announce:

More Increases To Our Taxes!

Yes, the answer they always seem to come up with is to steal more of our hard earned dollars. They cannot manage their budgets, so they force us to manage ours, by taking money out of our pockets!

Although tax rates vary by province, the following table illustrates the current combined Federal and highest Provincial income tax rates payable at various income levels, categorized by income type:

	$30,755 to $39,000	$39,001 to $61,509	$61,510 to $100,000	$100,001 and over
Salary & Interest	36.4%	42.4%	45.7%	48.6%
Dividends	23.8%	23.8%	31.3%	35.1%
Capital Gains	20.8%	20.8%	22.8%	24.3%

And that's just income tax. Governments have become more devious by devising new taxes and adding hidden taxes to increase revenues. As a Canadian, if you are in the top income bracket you could be paying as much as 75% of your income in some form of tax. Canadians know that income taxes are very high and represent a very large percentage of their annual tax bill. But, what many do not realize is that income tax may represent less than half of their total tax bill. These other and hidden taxes can account for over two-thirds of the average Canadian's total tax bill.

Let's look at the list of taxes we all have to pay:
1. Federal income and estate taxes.
2. Provincial income taxes
    a) Basic tax
    b) Flat tax
    c) Deficit-reduction tax
3. Corporate Income Taxes.
4. Payroll taxes.
5. G.S.T.
6. Provincial sales taxes.
7. Real estate property taxes.
8. Personal property taxes.
9. School taxes.
10. Business taxes.
11. Gasoline taxes.
12. Import duty taxes.
13. Sin taxes. (Cigarettes, Liquor, etc.)
14. Travel taxes. (Hotel, Airline, etc.)
15. Excise taxes.
16. Road taxes.
17. Utility surcharge taxes.

18. Environmental levy Taxes.
19. Air Travelers Security Taxes.
    And the list goes on and on.

As you look down the list of taxes, you may think that there are some that don't affect you, notably corporate income tax. However, don't be deceived, corporate income taxes are not really paid by corporations. They are passed on in the prices we all have to pay for their goods and services.

Not only does this list of taxes keep getting longer, the rates keep getting higher as well. The total tax bill of the average Canadian has increased by 1,351% since 1961, according to *Tax Facts 12*, the latest edition of a biennial study, which looks at how the average Canadian tax bill has changed since 1961.

Canadians Now Pay More Tax Than Citizens of any Other G7 Country!

The G7 countries are France, Japan, Germany, United States, Britain, Italy, and Canada.

Furthermore, according to the *Economic Freedom of the World: 2001 Annual Report* released April 19, 2001 by The Fraser Institute, Canada has dropped to number thirteen on the list of most economically free jurisdictions in the world. The report also says, "Comparatively speaking, Canada continues to have damagingly high levels of government spending, transfers and subsidies, and tax rates". Are you wondering which countries make up the top ten? Hong Kong (1), Singapore (2), New Zealand (3), the United Kingdom (4), the United States (5), Australia (6), Ireland (7), Switzerland (8), Luxembourg (9), and the Netherlands (10).

It's finally happening. Canadians are now actually quite angry about taxes. As a whole we're too politically correct to express a direct anger against taxation. However, a poll conducted in February 1999 by Compas (center for market and survey research) found that 85% of Canadians felt that taxes were too high. More than 70% of Canadians agreed with the following statements "Our tax levels do harm by discouraging business investment" and "Taxes cause many of our brightest young people to go elsewhere." In a March 2002 poll, surveying Canadian business leaders, they blame more than a third of our country's lower productivity on high taxation and 66% of those surveyed said they believe that "high taxes cause pervasive harm and are impediments to corporate growth".

Politicians on the other hand blame business and industry for lower productivity. Deputy Prime Minister John Manley said on March 13, 2002, "I worry that too many Canadian firms are profiting mightily from a 62-cent dollar and would be hard pressed to compete at an 80-cent dollar". It never even dawns on these dim wits that **TAX** is a major factor in competing with other businesses on the international markets. John Manley is the same politician who, while holding the portfolio of Canada's Industry Minister, said, "High tax levels increase productivity because it drives innovation in order to lower other costs" —National Post - December 5, 1998. Where in the world has this ever been proven? They just don't get it!

The tax situation is truly disgusting. Especially because the lack of leadership has placed the average Canadian in a position that we all hate, feeling bad about our country. Maybe George Burns was right, *"Too bad that all the people who really know how to run the country are busy driving taxi cabs and cutting hair"*.

We all know that Canada is still a great place on the planet to live and work. As messed up as we are, there are still many great opportunities here. That's why it feels so bad when we see our politicians taking away our incentives and the incentives of the next generation to earn, save and invest.

Let's take a look at how bad the situation is:

If you were to ask 100 people at the start of their working careers, "Do you believe you will be financially independent someday." I would be surprised if even one person answered "Not Me!"

However, 40 years later, according to Statistics Canada, only 1 will be wealthy; 8 will be financially secure; 14 will continue to work, not because they want to but because they need to; 24 will be dead; and 53 will be dead broke — dependent on their meager government benefit cheques, relatives, friends or even charity for a minimum standard of living.

That's 9% Who Are Successful And 91% Who Are Unsuccessful!

Any time a governmental body lacks the ability to run their affairs in a proper way; their answer is always the same:

Let's Tax Our Neighbors!

After all, they won't mind. We need the tax revenue to keep things going. Everybody has to pay his or her fair share! Right?

Give me a break. Let's talk about "paying your fair share."

♦ Is it fair that crown corporations get special mention in tax laws to reduce their tax burden?

♦ Is it fair that the federal government gave out $947 million in loans, and collected back just $24.4 million after seven years through a corporate welfare program know as Technology Partnerships Canada (TPC)?

♦ Is it fair that over a 16-year period the federal Department of Industry gave $11 billion to big business?

♦ Is it fair that, while they increase our taxes, elected Members of Parliament (MPs) get a yearly pension of 30% of their salary after only 6 years of service, payable immediately and for life? Or, that MPs receive a pension of 75% of their best 6 years after only 15 years? And, that these pensions are fully indexed for inflation?

♦ Is it fair that by creating new jobs, employers get to pay more payroll taxes? Payroll taxes have doubled since 1994.

♦ Is it fair that small business owners who take huge risks, sacrifice hours and hours of their time, create jobs, build better communities for us all, are then made "tax targets?"

♦ Is any of this fair? No, it sure isn't. The world is not always fair.

The world doesn't care about your personal situation. You won't get any medals for being successful. And you won't get yelled at for failing. All you will get is whatever you make of your life on your own.

How Can We Get Control?

Control is something that we all want, something that we all need.

You see, the lack of control makes us feel like we can't guide our lives the way we want to. Not being in control is scary. It's disturbing. It can feel very discouraging.

There are so many areas of our life where we don't have much, if any, control, which can cause us to feel a loss of peace of mind.

When you know you can steer your life in the direction you want, don't you enjoy each day a little more? Don't you sleep better at night? Don't you love your family just a little more?

Sure you do. That is why we all strive to work so hard. To gain more control.

And yes, having more money does provide more control.

And paying less in taxes puts more money in our pockets, which puts more control in our lives!

Yet, when you look at the long list of taxes we all have to pay, you will notice an interesting fact:

Of All The Taxes We Are Stuck With, Only A Couple Of Types Are Really Controllable!

Most of the taxes on the list are either built into the prices of things we pay, or added as a percentage of the value of something.

♦ If you want to buy some gasoline, you will pay the gasoline, road and sales taxes, without any option to get around them. 83% of the price of a litre of gasoline goes to government in the form taxes, royalties and charges.

♦ And how about a bottle of liquor. 81% of the cost of a bottle of liquor is tax or government mark-up, since they own the monopoly on alcohol sales.

♦ If you want to go on a trip, you will pay the airline, hotel taxes, and now the security tax, with zero say in the matter. And so on.

There are a couple of interesting exceptions to this "pay without choice" rule.

As a matter of fact, these exceptions are so big, that the fact they even exist is truly amazing. What am I talking about?

Federal And Provincial Income And Estate Taxes.

≫Chapter 2≪
God: "I Told You So."

"Of all tyrannies, a tyranny sincerely exercised for the good of its victims may be the most oppressive. It may be better to live under robber barons than under omnipotent moral busybodies. The robber baron's cruelty may sometimes sleep, his cupidity may at some point be satiated; but those who torment us for our own good will torment us without end, for they will do so with the approval of their own conscience." — C.S. Lewis (1898-1963)

What is the history of Taxation? Well, that's a book in itself and one I don't think would be very interesting to read. But, there are two historical points I'd like to illustrate. One tells that the current situation was predicted and the other gives a clue to the solution.

First the prediction — Approximately 1000 years B.C. the citizens of the nation of Israel were demanding to have a king. Samuel was the judge, or leader, of Israel at the time. All the other nations around Israel had kings and the people of Israel believed that they should have one too. Samuel wrote in First Samuel (the 9th book of the Bible) chapter 8 that he asked God what he should do about the people's request. According to what he wrote in that chapter, this is what God said would happen if the people of Israel allowed a king to reign over them:

> *"The king will draft your sons into his army and make them run before his chariots. Some will be commanders*

25

of his troops, while others will be slave laborers. Some will be forced to plow in his fields and harvest his crops, while others will make his weapons and chariot equipment. The king will take your daughters from you and force them to cook and bake and make perfumes for him. He will take away the best of your fields and vineyards and olive groves and give them to his servants. He will take a tenth of your harvest and distribute it among his officers and attendants. He will want your male and female slaves and demand the finest of your cattle and donkeys for his own use. He will demand a tenth of your flocks, and you will be his slaves. When that day comes, you will beg for relief from this king you are demanding, but the LORD will not help you."

Meanwhile 3000 years later, we **wish** the "king" would take only 10% instead of 50-75% of our income. The average Canadian is now a **slave** to the Government for a least half of the year. Even oppressed serfs only had to pay 20%. According to The Fraser Institute, the average Canadian family earns $51,174 and pays $24,309 in various forms of taxes. That's 50% of their annual income.

Let's look at it another way. Today civilized people all over the world are horrified by the thought of human slavery. Yet Canadians willingly give over half of their income to government. If this isn't slavery, what is? Furthermore, "a good slave owner" would at least provide his slaves with the essentials of food, clothing and shelter. If we examine the financial health of the majority of Canadians today we'd find that at the end of the month they don't have any more than food, clothing and shelter — they're slaves. Examine your own situation: If you have nothing left at the end of the month after paying your bills you're a slave too! *In levying taxes and in shearing sheep, it is well to stop when you get down to the skin.* —Austin O'Malley

It's time we all fought back and insisted that the bureaucrats and politicians of this country grab a shovel and get a job rather than living life on the dole.

What is the history of taxation in Canada? As you probably know, income taxes have been around for a long time. Originally, income tax was established in 1917 as a temporary measure to fund Canada's effort in World War I. But give government a taste, and they become addicted, and so temporary became de facto permanent. What's interesting to note is that if the original exemption (the amount of income you can earn **TAX-FREE**) had been increased with inflation, the exemption in 2000 would have been $18,044, instead of only $7,231.

Over the years, not surprisingly, the tax system has become very complicated. Progressive tax rates, deductions, credits, surcharges, allowances all contribute to the complexity of the system. The way we are taxed keeps changing each year too. Besides generating revenue for government, taxes are manipulated to encourage or discourage certain behaviors. So, if you take advantage of these incentives you're just doing exactly what the government is encouraging you and every

27

other Canadian to do. You could say that the government uses the taxation of our income and estates as a **"carrot and stick"** in an attempt to direct our financial lives. So you see, when you take advantage of the incentives contained in the tax laws to reduce your tax liability, you're just doing exactly what the government wants. You are not abusing the laws or exploiting any loopholes.

So, since they use these taxes to push us one way or another, a very interesting result has been created:

Taxes Can Be Significantly Changed Up Or Down, By The Way You Arrange Your Financial Affairs!

Think about that. It's incredible. You can literally decide how much in estate and income taxes you pay, based on decisions you make with your money. There isn't any other area of taxation that allows you such flexibility. Or that can cause you so much grief, if you set yourself up wrong.

And, yes, you can set yourself up the right way, much easier than you might think.

What is the "right way"? My definition of the "the right way" is paying the least amount of taxes of anybody in the same income bracket. Yes, that's right, two families can have the exact same income, and one can pay way less in taxes — a lot less. Let me give you an example:

Al and Susan earn the same amount of income as their in-laws, Dan and Mary. They both have houses in the same price range, in the same neighborhood, and have the same number of kids.

They work for the same company, and have the same company benefits available to them. As a matter of fact, they are the same in almost all respects, except for one.

Al and Susan pay several thousand dollars less than Dan and Mary in income taxes. That extra money has been used for years to build up enough money to pay for their children's education and to buy all kinds of investments for retirement and to go on nice vacations. And so on.

Dan and Mary have no idea how they will pay for college or retire or reach any of their goals.

How can this be? Well, it's because Al and Susan have taken advantage of the tax laws and Dan and Mary have never bothered. They thought they were too busy, or that Revenue Canada would hang them, or that the "incentives" weren't for them, or a thousand other excuses.

Excuses don't put money in your pocket. Don't let anything or anyone stop you from using every strategy available to you to reduce your taxes. Don't listen to the well meaning, less informed, friend or advisor who is only too happy to tell you that it can't be done. It can be done and it must be done. Only careful planning of your finances to reduce taxes can put money right where it belongs, in your pocket!

Don't Overpay!

What kinds of things can you do?
Well... go to Section 2 - The 10 Secrets.

Section 2
–The 10 Secrets–

(Note: The strategies explained in The 10 Secrets... do work. However, you should not run out and do any, or all of them, without proper counsel from a qualified tax advisor/financial planner! It will be necessary to coordinate all of your financial issues to make sure you are making the right moves. Tax planning cannot be done in a vacuum. You must tie together all of the pieces of the puzzle!)

What's the secret to not over paying your taxes? Throughout this section of the book I will outline various ideas, strategies and planning opportunities for reducing tax. To help you remember, I have created an acronym to give a framework to the concepts involved in tax planning. The secret to paying less tax is S-E-C-R-E-T.

S-E-C-R-E-T

S is for **SPLIT**. Income splitting is a strategy that involves transferring a portion of income from someone who is in a high tax bracket to someone who is in a lower tax bracket. It may even be possible to reduce the tax on the transferred income to zero if the person, who it is being transferred to, doesn't have any other taxable income. Normally, the other person is either your spouse or common-law spouse, but it could even be your children. Whenever it is possible to transfer income to someone in a lower tax bracket, it should be done. If the difference between tax rates is 20% then your family will save $200 for every $1,000 transferred to the "lower rate" family member.

E is for **ELIMINATE.** Eliminate as much tax as possible by maximizing your deductions and tax credits. Throughout *The 10 Secrets* I will be making references to tax deductions and tax credits. The following should define and clarify the difference and the effects of a deduction and a credit:

♦ A tax **deduction,** or "write off" as it's sometimes called, reduces your taxable income, by allowing you to subtract the amount of an expense from your income, before calculating how much tax you must pay. The more or higher the deductions, the lower your taxable income. Also, the more you reduce your taxable income the less exposure you will have to the higher tax rates in the higher income brackets, because Canada's tax scheme is a progressive one. Which means the more you earn the higher the tax rate. For example: Lowering your taxable income from $40,000 to $39,000 would save you almost $424 in tax. Therefore, the higher your income bracket the more valuable a deduction is to you.

♦ A tax **credit** on the other hand is a direct reduction of the actual tax you pay. A $100 tax credit is worth $100 to you no matter how much income you earn. A tax credit is a direct reduction of tax payable.

C is for **CLAIM.** Claim everything you are allowed to claim to reduce your taxes to the least amount possible. You may have heard it said that there are degrees of legitimacy to claiming expenses. These are sometimes characterized as black and white, or grey areas. Some tax planners suggest that you stay as far away from the line as possible so that you don't get into trouble with Revenue Canada. Other more aggressive planners suggest that you take advantage of everything that is legal, even pushing the limits of permissibility. I prefer the aggressive approach; because the worst that can happen if you're wrong, is that you may have an expense disallowed. But if you don't try, you'll never know whether you could have been successful at paying less tax, and you'll just have to fork over more of your hard earned money. Look at it another way, if you missed including a deduction that you're entitled to, Revenue Canada won't remind you. Will they?

R is for **REARRANGE**. Rearrange whatever you have to, to lower your tax bill. Some examples include:

♦ Change your income from a type that is fully taxed to one that is only partially taxed or **TAX-FREE**.

♦ Chose investments that have a preferred tax treatment. Income from different kinds of investments is taxed at different rates.

♦ Shift some of your income from a year that you'll be in a high tax bracket to a year when you'll be in a lower tax bracket.

♦ Defer or postpone paying taxes. Use strategies and investment vehicles to put off paying tax now. Don't pay today what you can pay tomorrow. Give yourself the time use of your money. The longer you can put off paying a tax the longer you have the use of your money for your purposes.

E is for **EXPATRIATE**. Utilize offshore strategies. It is estimated that there is $5 trillion dollars invested offshore, approximately one-third of the world's wealth. Although this idea may require significant planning, there may be opportunities outside of Canada for you to invest, do business or even retire, that can give you significant tax saving benefits.

T is for **TAX SHELTERS**. There can be risks associated with investing in some tax shelters. Nevertheless, a good tax shelter can give you the opportunity to watch your invested money grow while delaying or eliminating the tax that might have to be paid if it were invested outside of the shelter. A complete understanding of the investment and advice from a competent advisor is a must. No matter how good something sounds don't get involved until you understand it. Too many people have lost fortunes by not sticking to the most important rule of investing. The number one rule of investing is:

Never Invest In Anything You Don't Understand!

Now you know the **S-E-C-R-E-T** to paying less tax. The following **10 Secrets** will show you ways to **S**plit income, **E**liminate taxes by maximizing deductions and credits, **C**laim what is within your right, **R**earrange your assets and/or income, **E**xpatriate, and use **T**ax shelters to reduce or eliminate your tax bill!

There is one final principle that I feel I need to explain before we explore *The 10 Secrets...*, that is compound interest and/or the "compounding" effect. Throughout the 10 secrets I will refer to the term compound interest or compound effect. It is important to understand the benefit of compounding. Although you may understand it, unfortunately many people do not.

Regular or simple interest is calculated on the amount of money you have invested and is paid out to you at regular intervals. Compound interest on the other hand is not paid out. Rather it is added to you initial investment. Then the next time interest is earned it is calculated on the total of your initial investment and any built up interest that you've already earned. Your interest earns interest. This compounding effect can have significant benefits to you over time. The more often your investment compounds the faster it grows.

$10,000 invested at 10% simple interest would be worth $20,000 after 10 years. However, $10,000 invested at 10% compound interest would be worth $25,937.42 after 10 years because the interest paid was added to the investment each year. From the second compounding period on, your interest was earning interest too.

There's a rule that you can use to figure out how many years it will take for your money to double using compound interest. The rule is called, the rule of 72. Divide the interest rate that your money is earning into the number 72. The result will be the number of years it take for you to double your money.

If you are earning 10% interest it will take 7.2 years for your money to double, but if you're only earning 5% interest (half lost to the tax man) it will take 14.4 years for your money to double. Money lost to the tax man this year can have far reaching effects for years to come. Therefore, it is so important to reduce your tax to as low as possible and to do it now!

Thinking is one thing no one has even been able to tax.
—Charles Kettering, scientist, inventor (1876-1958)

⮄Secret 1⮃
Take Maximum Advantage Of Your RRSP

You hear a lot about registered retirement savings plans (RRSPs) every February because the deadline for contributing to an RRSP, for the previous tax year, is 60 days from the start of the year. March 1 on non leap years and February 29 on leap years. You hear so much about RRSPs because it's big business and all the financial institutions are competing for their share of the $250 billion dollar pool of RRSP cash. RRSPs are the most widely used tax shelter in Canada.

There are many good RRSP reference books available at your local bookstore. The shelves are filled with them each year during January and February. They give detailed information about all the limits, rules, types, and exit strategies of RRSPs. For this reason I won't go into detail, in this chapter, about how they work, how much you can contribute, etc., etc. Instead, my primary purpose of having a chapter on RRSPs in this book is because of their tax deferral benefits. Also I want to point out some of the lesser-known ways of taking advantage of your RRSP and to make you aware of mistakes that people make with their RRSPs.

Tax Deferral Investment Vehicle
An RRSP is simply a tax deferral investment vehicle. Which means that an RRSP allows you, within limits, to put

some of your "earned" income into an investment, and not have to pay tax now on that income. Everything you put into an RRSP and all the interest that it earns is not taxed until you withdraw it.

Suppose you earn $45,000, Revenue Canada says you'll have to pay a tax of $11,424 on your income. But if you decide to put $10,000 into an RRSP you won't have to pay tax on that portion of your income now. You will be allowed to make a deduction ("write-off") from your income of the $10,000. Because, of your lower "taxable" income and the lower income tax bracket, Revenue Canada says they'll be satisfied with a tax bill of $7,874. You'll enjoy a tax saving equal to $3,550. And now the $10,000 that you invested is working for you in an investment that will not be taxed until you take the money out.

Further, let's suppose that you invested $10,000 each year for 20 years in an RRSP that was earning 10% per year. At the end of the 20 years you'd have $630,025. If on the other hand, you invested the $10,000 in an investment that was not sheltered from tax, and you paid tax on the income before investing it and paid tax each year on the investment earnings, you would only have $181,362. Let's examine why. First, if you paid tax on the $10,000, you would only have $5,140 dollars to invest. Secondly, if you paid tax on the annual investment earnings, you would only be earning the equivalent of 5.14% instead of 10%.

Now remember that when you take money out of your RRSP it is taxed, so if you took all the money out at the end of 20 years you'd be taxed $306,192 (at today's rates) and you'd be left with $323,833. That's $142,471 more than you'd have if you did not use an RRSP!

But that's only part of the story. You are only taxed on the amount of money you take out of your RRSP. Proper planning would give you an income flow from your RRSP funds over many years while sheltering the rest of your money from immediate taxation. A good financial planner can help you plan this income taking into consideration all the many options, plans, and income vehicles available to you at the time you wish to start taking money out of you plan.

Remember, although an RRSP is a tax deferral tool that gives you immediate tax planning benefits, its real benefit is the opportunity to shelter future investment income. The best part of an RRSP is its tax-sheltered compound growth that will take place over the years to come!

Now let's examine some of the strategies and mistakes some people make when investing in RRSPs:

♦ **The RRSP Home Buyers Plan.** Because an RRSP is, strictly speaking, a tax deferral vehicle you can use it for deferring income now and use it later for things other than retirement. Although this will reduce the amount of money you have at retirement, you can use it to subsidize your income in years that you have a lower income or may have lost your job. You can also use an RRSP to defer income to purchase a home. The plan allows first-time homebuyers to withdraw up to $20,000 **TAX-FREE** from their RRSP as long as you pay it back in installments over the next 15 years. If you are a couple, you can each withdraw $20,000 from each of your RRSPs, which will give you $40,000 to purchase a home.

♦ **The Lifelong Learning Plan**. Again, as with the home buyers' plan, we can see another way to take maximum advantage of your RRSP. You can access funds from your RRSP to help pay for your own, or your spouse's, education. Under the Lifelong Learning Plan (LLP), you have the right to withdraw up to $10,000 per year without paying tax, to a maximum of $20,000 over a 4-year period. Then to avoid having to pay tax on the money you used for education, you must repay the money over a 10-year period starting after the fifth year.

♦ **Contribute as early in the year as possible**. If you contribute at the start of the year, all of the income earned will accumulate tax-sheltered. The effect of early contributions over a few years will be incredible. If you've always made your contribution just before the deadline, consider making both a contribution for the current year and next year at the same time. Then continue as usual, making your contributions at the "deadline" — only then you'll always be one year ahead.

Example: Suppose you annually contribute $10,000 to your RRSP. The difference between making your contribution at the beginning of the year rather than at the end of the year, over 30 years at 10% interest per year, would be $164,494.

♦ **Contribute anyway**. If you have the money to make a contribution. But, don't want to claim the deduction in the current year because you are already in a low-income position, make the contribution but delay the deduction. You can claim the deduction in a later year. This way, if you know your income will be higher in future years, you can maximize the tax-sheltered growth of your money now while maximizing you tax savings later.

♦ **Put your interest earning investments into your RRSP.** If your portfolio consists of investments that earn interest such as GICs and bonds, and investments that earn capital gains and dividends such as growth funds, consider putting your interest earning investments into your RRSP. This way you can reduce your exposure to tax, because until you sell your investment fund shares you will not have to pay much tax on their annual income. But, interest income is taxed at your highest rate of tax, annually.

Note: This strategy doesn't mean that your RRSP should not own growth investments, only that if you now own interest earning investments outside of your RRSP this is one very good way to shelter them.

♦ **Transfer your retiring allowance or severance pay to your RRSP.** There are limits, but you can shelter the lump sum payments you receive when you retire or leave your employment, in your RRSP. You can include retiring allowances, sick leave credits, severance pay, or a payment for wrongful dismissal. This could provide very significant income benefits for you at retirement, while allowing you a large tax deduction now. Otherwise you might find yourself giving Revenue Canada the largest part of your severance package.

♦ **Name your spouse as beneficiary or lose half of your RRSP.** Upon your death the entire amount of your RRSP will be added to your income in the year you die **UNLESS** you have named your spouse or dependent child as a beneficiary. Your spouse can then put the funds into his/her RRSP without incurring any tax. If you make the mistake of not naming a beneficiary and your estate wasn't in the highest tax bracket the day before you died, it will be the day after. Which means: Revenue Canada just inherited more of your RRSP than your spouse or children.

♦ **Maximize your foreign content.** It is important to have the maximum percentage of foreign investments allowed in your RRSP. Why? There are two main reasons:

1) There are often greater investment opportunities outside of Canada that will allow you to earn greater rates of return on your investment. And

2) Canada's continually devaluing currency means that the buying power of the Canadian dollars in you RRSP will buy less and less.

The rule is that you can now hold up to 30% of your RRSP in foreign investments. But, there are a couple of strategies to increase your actual foreign content above 30% with out being penalized. A financial planner can help you put these strategies in place; however, one way to take advantage of this is to have your RRSP invest in a Canadian investment that invests in foreign investments. Revenue Canada will consider this to be Canadian content even though the vehicle you invested in is holding foreign investments. RRSP experts such as Gordon Pape believe that the desired ratio of foreign content in your RRSP should be between 40% and 60%. Considering the current financial shape that the government of Canada is in, how much money do you want invested in Canada?

♦ **Contribute to a spousal RRSP.** You will recall at the beginning of Section 2, I wrote about the benefits of splitting your income to save tax. Well, contributing to a spousal RRSP is an income splitting strategy. Any amount that you are allowed to contribute to a regular RRSP may be contributed to a spousal RRSP. A spousal RRSP is an RRSP that is in the name of your spouse but where you still get to use the deduction to reduce your current year's "taxable" income. The advantage of a spousal RRSP is that at retirement, if your spouse will be in a lower tax bracket than you, he or she will be able to take income from the RRSP at a considerable tax saving. It is possible that your spouse may be in a tax bracket that is 20 percentage points lower than yours. Therefore, this is a strategy not to be over looked.

♦ **If you're going to retire outside of Canada.** When you leave Canada you are not required to collapse your RRSP. It can continue to grow tax-sheltered. Normally when you take money from your RRSP, you would be taxed at the highest tax rate bracket when you combine your income and the withdrawal from your RRSP. This rate could be as high as 48.6%. However, if you plan on retiring outside of Canada, wait until you are a nonresident and then make withdrawals from your RRSP. This way the maximum it will cost you is the withholding tax of 25%. It could even be less depending on the tax treaty Canada has with the country you take up residence in.

Another way to minimize the tax on money taken from your RRSP is to take a series of smaller payments. As long as you only take withdrawals of up to $5,000 at a time, the withholding tax that your financial institution is required to take and send to Revenue Canada is just 10%. Therefore, it is possible as a non-resident to exhaust your RRSP over time at a cost of only 10%.

Note: This strategy is not effective for Canadian residents since Revenue Canada will just get even with you next year by including your RRSP withdrawals in your total income for the year.

♦ **Pay fees directly.** There can be fees associated with your RRSP such as administration and trustee fees charged by the institution that manages your RRSP. Tell them you want to pay these fees directly. Although you cannot use these fees as deductions, if the fees are paid from your RRSP it will erode the amount of money that you have growing **TAX-FREE** in your RRSP. If you pay $250 per year in fees from your RRSP (averaging an annual return of 10%) you will have almost $27,000 less in your RRSP in 25 years. Sometimes a small mistake can add up to be a costly one.

WARNING - A government that spends money without accountability (they just arrogantly ignore the Auditor General whenever asked to account for their waste) and that is constantly searching for new sources of money cannot be trusted. P.J. O'Rourke said, *"Giving money and power to government is like giving whiskey and car keys to teenage boys."* A law or agreement today may be changed or broken in the future.

Over the last 20 years there has been many discussions about whether RRSPs will ever be taxed or even partially taxed. Therefore, it is with a word of caution that I say, almost everyone should have an RRSP. However, it is my firm belief that if you rely completely on only your RRSP for retirement you may, some day in the future, be sorry. For this reason it is important to discuss all investment options with your financial planner.

In general, the art of government consists of taking as much money as possible from one class of citizens to give to the other.
—Voltaire, philosopher, historian, and essayist (1694-1778)

When plunder has become a way of life for a group of people living together in society, they create for themselves in the course of time a legal system that authorizes it, and a moral code that glorifies it.
—Frederic Bastiat, economist (1801-1850)

◌ Secret 2 ◌
Overpaying Withholding Taxes Is A Big Mistake

This is one of the best-kept secrets of all. Revenue Canada makes billions of dollars each year because Canadians willingly or unknowingly overpay their withholding taxes. This is the tax that is taken off most Canadians cheques by their employers before they even see it. The reason the secret is so well kept is that Revenue Canada would love to have you continue overpaying and no other organization has a vested interest in seeing you stop.

Imagine you own a business that allows you to withdraw sums of money directly from your customer's bank accounts each month of the year without having to determine what they really owe you. Then after the end of each year, you make a formula available to them, so that they can calculate how much they really should have paid. Following that, if they feel that they have over paid, they can apply to you for a refund.

Rhetorical Questions:

1. How would you like to own a business like this?

2. How would you like to be a customer of this business?

3. If you were a customer of this business, would you willingly send them more money each month than you absolutely had to?

47

Obviously no one would give more of his or her money than was absolutely necessary. But each year Canadians give Revenue Canada billions of dollars in overpayments.

How big of a deal is this overpayment of withholding taxes anyway? Each year Revenue Canada handles approximately 21 million tax returns, of which over 12 million (59%) are owed an average refund of approximately $1,000. The total of these refunds is in excess of $12 billion dollars. That means that

Each Year Revenue Canada Holds On To $12 Billion Dollars That Doesn't Belong To Them.

Revenue Canada collects approximately $100 billion each year through the income tax. If they have to give $12 billion of refunds then 12% of the money they collected was never theirs in the first place.

If you have money in your possession that doesn't belong to you, isn't that called THEFT? The only difference is that the taxpayers allowed it to happen voluntarily.

Let's take this example a little further. At 6% interest, if Revenue Canada is holding $12 Billion dollars of overpaid withholding taxes, that represents $720 million dollars of lost interest. That's investment income that could have been earned by the Canadians who the money actually belongs to. Now you know why Revenue Canada doesn't want you to know this SECRET!

Here are several planning opportunities for reducing your withholding taxes:

♦ First, you should review the TD1 form that you filed with your employer. Make sure you correct any errors or omissions that may be costing you money. Although the form has its limitations, there are areas that can save you money. For example, you may have originally completed the form as single with no dependents, but now you may have a dependent spouse and child. This change alone could significantly increase your pay cheque.

♦ Second, whether you pay source withholdings (employer) or installments (self employed or retired), you can apply to your local Revenue Canada office to allow you to reduce your withholding tax for deductions or credits not covered by the TD1 form. These would include RRSP contributions, medical expenses, charitable contributions, etc. Get a waiver form from Revenue Canada and give it to your employer, then he or she will be released of responsibility in reducing your payroll taxes and can give you a bigger pay cheque each month.

These strategies allow you to have your tax savings NOW to spend and invest as you see fit, rather than waiting for a tax refund. Remember, a refund is just the return of your own money that you never owed in the first place.

How will this strategy impact you personally? Let's look at an example: Say you become a good student of tax reduction and you have set yourself up to save $4,800 in taxes for this year. If you keep your withholdings at the same level, you will get a big refund next year. This "loan" that you would be making to Revenue Canada is free of interest. Revenue Canada won't pay you one dime for the use of your money! PLUS, it will cost you several hundred dollars of lost interest that you will never see.

On the other hand, by changing your withholding tax, you end up getting $400 per month extra take home pay, NOW, which you can invest to earn interest! $400 per month invested at a 10% annual rate of return is equal to $2,550,712 over 40 years, the length of the average working lifetime.

You are allowed under the law to only withhold the amount of taxes you expect to pay. Actually, you can even be a little short and you won't even get a penalty when you pay the balance with your return.

Many Canadians fear having to pay Revenue Canada an additional tax payment along with their tax return in April. So they make sure this never happens, by overpaying their withholding taxes throughout the year. In fact, I've had people tell me that they like overpaying their withholdings as a forced savings program, and then looking forward to receiving a large refund in spring. But I suggest to you, if you end up each year owing a couple hundred dollars more than you had already sent to Revenue Canada, instead of waiting for a significant refund, then you're the real winner.

Better In Your Pocket Than Theirs.

If you want a forced savings account, go to your bank or your financial planner and ask him or her to take a pre-authorized amount out of your chequing account each month and deposit into an investment account.

Never, ever give Revenue Canada money that is yours. Always remember, it's not their money and a refund is not a nice gift at the end of the year, it's just a return of your money that they had no right to. Never be afraid of doing what the law allows!

Never Let Them Steal Your Hard Earned Money!

The fact is that government, like a highwayman, says to a man: "Your money or your life." And many, if not most, taxes are paid under the compulsion of that threat. The government does not, indeed, waylay a man in a lonely place, spring upon him from the roadside, and, holding a pistol to his head, proceed to rifle his pockets. But the robbery is none the less a robbery on that account; and it is far more dastardly and shameful.
—Lysander Spooner (1808-1887)

⁓ Secret 3 ⁓
Earn Dividends
Instead Of Interest

There are 3 types of income that can be earned from an investment. They are interest, dividends and capital gains. Each type is generated differently and is taxed differently, as you can see from the chart below.

	$30,755 to $39,000	$39,001 to $61,509	$61,510 to $100,000	$100,001 and over
Salary & Interest	36.4%	42.4%	45.7%	48.6%
Dividends	23.8%	23.8%	31.3%	35.1%
Capital Gains	20.8%	20.8%	22.8%	24.3%

Let's examine each type of income in more depth:

Interest

Interest is a payment made by a borrower to a lender for the use of the lenders money. Interest earning investments can take many different forms. A promissory note; a certificate of deposit or guarantee investment certificate (GIC) from a bank or trust company; a treasury bill or bond issued by a government; or a corporate bond issued by a business, are all examples of interest bearing investments. When you purchase an investment such as a GIC you are loaning your money to the bank. They in turn pay rent on your money in the form of interest. Taxation of interest income is treated the same way as employment income. As you can see from the tax chart, tax on interest income is charged the highest rate.

Dividend

A dividend is a payment made to a shareholder of a corporation from the after tax profits earned by the company from their business activities. Dividends are earned from ownership of common and preferred shares. However, preferred shareholders have first claim on the assets of the company in the event of its bankruptcy. They also have first claim on the annual dividend payments. Also, unlike common shares, with preferred shares, management is required to pay a dividend, and the amount is predetermined — for example, $5 per share. Management is committed to pay the dividend in much the same way it is required to pay interest on debt. Therefore, you could say that preferred shares are more or less a cross between common shares and a bond. Or, another way to look at it, preferred shares are stocks that act like bonds. Taxation of dividend income is given special treatment. Since the corporation has already paid it's tax before giving you your portion of the profit by way of a dividend, you pay less tax on the dividend income than you would on an interest payment.

Capital Gain

A capital gain is the amount that the value of your investment has increased since it was purchased. You "realize" a capital gain when you sell the investment. A capital gain is the difference between the amount you paid to purchase an investment, and the price you sell it for. For tax purposes the cost (amount you paid for the investment) is referred to as the adjusted cost base (ACB). Capital gains have the least amount of tax as you can see from the chart. That's because only 50%

of the gain is taxable. You get to earn half of all your capital gains **TAX-FREE!**

Capital gains are unique in another way. Unlike interest and dividend income, which are paid out and taxed each year, capital gains are sheltered from tax until the asset is sold. This is referred to as "unrealized" capital gain. Because of the low tax rates, it would make sense to earn only capital gains income if it were possible. However, if you make your living from buying and selling capital property, Revenue Canada may decide that they will treat your capital gains as personal or business income and tax you at the maximum rate.

One exception to the taxation of capital gains is the capital gains realized on the sale of your personal residence. Your personal residence is a permanent tax shelter. You can buy and sell your personal residence for a **TAX-FREE** profit once per year. If you are in a market with escalating real estate prices or you know how to spot bargains or like to buy and improve properties, this may be a way for you to earn a significant amount of your income **TAX-FREE.**

In examination of the income strategies available to the majority of Canadians to reduce tax over the long term, it would seem that changing investments from interest earning investments to dividend earning investments gives us the greatest planning opportunities. And it is also the easiest.

Canadians tend to be ultra-conservative investors; often limiting their portfolios to interest earning investments such as guaranteed investment certificates (GICs) and bonds. However, as we have seen, converting your interest earning investments into dividend earning investments has huge tax benefits and this is a very low-risk, safe strategy.

How can you do it? By buying preferred shares, or by investing in an investment fund that holds preferred shares. People, who have always been comfortable depositing money with banks in exchange for interest, may now consider purchasing bank shares instead. This way you can earn a piece of the billion dollar profits earned each year by Canadian banks.

Let's look specifically at how changing your investments from interest earning to dividend earning can benefit you tax wise. If you're in the top income tax bracket, you'll pay only 35.1% tax on a dividend payment, while if you earned the same amount as an interest payment you'd have to pay 48.6%, as you can see from the chart. That's a tax reduction of 13.5 percentage points, which represents a 28% tax savings.

If you're taxable income is between $39,000 and $61,509 the benefit, of earning dividends instead of interest, is even greater. The tax chart illustrates that the tax rate in this bracket, on interest income, is 42.4% while the tax rate on dividends is only 23.8%. Therefore, by earning dividend income, you would reduce your tax rate by 18.6 percentage points.

That's a 44% Tax Saving!

Put another way, if you earned $20,000 in interest from GICs last year and you moved your investment into a dividend earning investment, next year you'd have an extra $3,720 to spend or reinvest, assuming exactly the same rate of return. Depending on how extravagant a traveler you are, that might be enough to take a nice vacation. Or, you could reinvest the $3,720 that you'll be saving. By reinvesting, you could grow your savings into a very substantial investment. Assuming you reinvested the $3,720 each year for the next 20 years at an annual yield of 10%, you'd have $213,000. Two hundred thousand dollars to do whatever you want with, just by taking advantage of this one secret!

Tax-Free Income!

And finally, if you receive only dividend income, it is possible to earn all, or at least a significant amount, of your income **TAX-FREE**. Depending on the province that you live in, you could earn up to $28,670 of dividend income **TAX-FREE**; although the tax rate chart at the beginning of this chapter does not illustrate this, because it starts at an income bracket of $30,755. This is possible because of the basic personal and dividend tax credit, and the way that the tax rates are calculated. The amount that you can earn **TAX-FREE** is different in each province due to different provincial tax rates and dividend tax credits. Here is the amount of dividends that can be earned **TAX-FREE** in your province:

British Columbia	$28,230
Alberta	$28,670
Saskatchewan	$22,160
Manitoba	$10,960
Ontario	$27,990
Quebec	$18,270
New Brunswick	$25,470
Nova Scotia	$24,710
Prince Edward Island	$25,660
Newfoundland	$27,240

Source: KPMG - *Tax Facts 2001-2002*

To restructure your portfolio and to determine the amount you can earn **TAX-FREE** in your province talk with your tax advisor/financial planner.

∞ Secret 4 ∞
Make Your Mortgage Interest Tax Deductible

Your home is one of the last permanent tax shelters left in Canada. There are no capital gains taxes on the sale of principle residences in Canada. This provides a great opportunity to shelter **TAX-FREE** profit in your home. Take note that although we generally think of a principle residence as a house, for the purposes of tax a principle residence can be a house, apartment, condominium, duplex, cottage, mobile home trailer or a houseboat.

In addition to the **TAX-FREE** capital gain of a principle residence, there is an incredible opportunity to make what is many people's single largest annual expense, tax deductible. That expense being the interest you pay on your mortgage! All it takes is some planning and you will save substantial taxes.

In the past while examining a person's assets and liabilities on their net worth statement, I have noticed that they had an investment portfolio totaling more than the balance of their mortgage. Herein lies the opportunity.

If you have a mortgage on your home and an investment portfolio equal to or greater than your mortgage, then you should cash in your investments and use the money to pay off your mortgage.

Then you can borrow new funds secured by a new mortgage to buy back new investments for your investment portfolio. The interest that you will be paying on your new mortgage will now be tax deductible.

Why do you have to go through all this hassle to make it happen? Well, Revenue Canada says that all the interest you pay on money you've borrowed to make investments is tax deductible. However, if you borrowed money to purchase a home that interest is not tax deductible. That's why you have to go through the whole process. In the end, you'll have borrowed money to invest and put your home up as security. That makes it tax deductible.

WARNING - You must do this properly or Revenue Canada may use something they call the general anti-avoidance rule on you. This would have the effect of disallowing your interest deduction. Making the whole exercise useless.

♦ Make certain that the new mortgage was needed by the bank to secure your loan to buy investments

♦ Do not purchase the exact same investments you held prior to paying off your mortgage. You should purchase new investments.

EXAMPLE: Suppose you have a $100,000 mortgage and $100,000 worth of maturing GICs. Take the cash from the GICs and pay off your mortgage. Then get a new mortgage and use the funds to purchase preferred shares or place the money in a dividend investment fund. Now your mortgage interest is tax deductible and you would have legitimized the effort by buying new investments (preferred shares instead of GICs).

Depending on the interest rate that you're able to negotiate with your bank, this will give an annual tax deduction of between $6,500 - $9,500. If you're in a 50% tax bracket the cash value of this strategy is equal to half of the deduction, so a $8,000 deduction is equivalent to putting $4,000 right into your pocket. You're paying the interest now anyway, so do this and put the cash back in your pocket!

This is a WIN-WIN situation — You make your mortgage interest tax deductible and convert your highly taxed interest earning investments into tax-preferred dividend paying investments.

Opportunity For Small Business Owners

Although business owners as well as non-business owners may use the strategy above, the following strategy is exclusively for business owners.

Question: Do you have a shareholder's loan that is greater than or equal to the balance of your home mortgage? If so, then by creating a fairly simple paper trail you can make your mortgage interest, tax-deductible.

Here's the process:
1. Your small business corporation takes a loan from the bank, equal to your shareholder's loan.
2. The corporation then uses the borrowed funds to pay out your shareholder's loan. This money is **TAX-FREE** in your hands.
3. You then use these funds to pay off the balance of your mortgage.
4. Then you take a new mortgage on your home and use the proceeds to invest in your company, creating a new shareholders loan.

61

5. Your company then uses these funds to repay the bank loan it made to pay you out in the first place (#1).

Now Your Mortgage Interest Is Tax-Deductible!

When a simple strategy, such as this one, is presented to them, business owners often get upset with their advisors, believing their advisors should have told them about the strategy. But, let's look at why that may not happen. Your accountant's responsibility is to keep track of the corporate financial statements and may not even know your personal mortgage situation. Your banker doesn't know whether or not you are already using your mortgage interest as a deduction. And, your mutual fund and life insurance agents may not understand these types of strategies unless they relate directly to the products they sell. Therefore, the only way you can stay on top of all the opportunities is to make sure you have a qualified, experienced financial planner working for you, asking the right questions.

This and no other is the root from which a tyrant springs; when he first appears he is a protector.
—Plato circa 400 B.C.

Public works are not accomplished by the miraculous power of a magic wand. They are paid for by funds taken away from the citizens.
—Ludwig von Mises, economist,
  professor (1881-1973)

We must remember that government, no matter how hard it tries, cannot protect individuals from themselves.
—Peter Calcagno, economics professor -
  Wingate University

ᨪ Secret 5 ᨪ
Render Unto Caesar [ONLY] The Things That Are Caesar's

It's written in the Biblical book of Matthew, chapter 22, verse 21, that Jesus said, "Render therefore unto Caesar the things which are Caesar's," referring to the paying of taxes. I'd like to add to that verse — Give him ONLY what is absolutely his and no more!

Never Give Them Any More Than You Have To!

This chapter is a collection of ideas, strategies and tax planning tips that you can use to maximize your deductions and credits. Although none of them required its own chapter to explain, they are all very good ways to reduce the tax you pay. Collectively they could save you thousands of dollars per year.

♦ **Deduct all business and investment losses.** Over the past 24 years Revenue Canada disallowed many investors deductions using a test called the "reasonable-expectation-of-profit" test. When in the Revenue Canada agent's opinion, the taxpayer did not 'expect' to make a profit; they used this test to disallow deductions that investors had claimed for investment losses.

Well, all that changed on May 23, 2002! The Supreme Court of Canada ruled that Revenue Canada has been misusing the "reasonable-expectation-of-profit" test. From now on the test can only be used to decide whether an investment is related to a hobby, personal activity or personal use. "Where the nature of an activity is clearly commercial, there is no need to analyze the taxpayer's business decisions," the court decided, adding that the test "should not be used to second-guess the business judgment of the taxpayer. It is the commercial nature of the taxpayer's activity which must be evaluated not his or her business acumen".

Now you can go ahead and write off your investment losses without fear of reprisal from Revenue Canada.

♦ **Write off your fines, tickets, levies, and penalties.** Revenue Canada in the past has disallowed many fines and penalties that taxpayers have claimed as deductions, stating that they were not legitimate expenses. Well, on April 20, 1999 another Supreme Court decision forced Revenue Canada to return taxes to a taxpayer, allowing the deduction of a fine. In the Supreme Court's decision they said, "Levies, fines, and penalties which are incurred for the purpose of earning income are deductible business expenses."

♦ **Take full advantage of the Child Tax Benefit.** As a parent, if you invest the monthly Child Tax Benefit payments, in your child's name, you will not be responsible for paying tax on the earnings of the investment. For tax purposes Revenue Canada views the child tax benefit as belonging to your child. So, any interest it earns also belongs to your child.

Over time, a significant investment can be built up. And, because the interest will likely never put the child in a taxable position, the earnings are **TAX-FREE.**

Example: Suppose you receive a Child Tax Benefit payment of $75.00 per month. $75.00 invested at 10% interest for 20 years equals $57,427.

For this reason I never recommend purchasing tax-sheltered or tax-deferred plans such as life insurance or registered education savings plans (RESP) with these funds. I'm not saying that you shouldn't purchase those types of plans for your children. Just don't use the Child Tax Benefit payment to do it. You could lose a significant benefit if you do, because when you take funds out of tax-sheltered plans the money becomes taxable. Outside of these plans it can all remain **TAX-FREE.**

♦ **Loan money to your children to build a college fund.** If your child earns income from a job, either over summer or throughout the year, you might want to make him or her an interest free loan, equal to what they earn. This allows the child to invest their employment income, so that the investment income they received will be taxable in their hands, not yours.

This is a great way to reduce the tax that you would have to pay on the earnings if you invested the money yourself for their college education. And, it also gives you a great hands-on forum to teach your children about investing.

Example: Suppose your son earns $5,000 over the summer and invests it. You then loan him $5,000 interest-free to make up for the fact that he invested all of his money. And, if you did that for 5 years, to build a college fund, at say 10% interest, he'd have $33,578.

♦ **Buy an equity investment fund in your child's name.** Revenue Canada has a rule that they call the attribution rule. This simply means that if you make an investment in your spouse's or your child's name for the purpose of sheltering the profit earned from that investment, from tax, Revenue Canada will attribute the income back to you anyway. There are a few exceptions. Interest and dividend income is attributed back to the donor; however, this rule doesn't apply to capital gains. You could invest in an equity investment fund in your child's name. The capital gains earned by the fund are taxable in your child's hands. But since taxes are only charged on realized capital gains, and then at a low rate, this is a great way to build a child's education fund.

♦ **Pay your spouse's taxes.** Another way to get around Revenue Canada's attribution rule, and split income with your lower income spouse, is to pay his or her taxes. If you paid your spouse's taxes, the payment would be viewed as a gift and therefore not taxable. The money he or she would have paid in taxes can then be invested. As the investment earns income it would be taxable in your spouse's hand rather than yours.

Suppose you pay a $5,000 tax bill for your spouse each year and he or she invested that amount into an investment earning 10% annually over a period of 10 years, there would be $87,656 in it at the end of the 10 years. The tax savings at that point, if your spouse's tax rate was say 20% less than yours, could be equal to $2,000 per year. And as the investment grows the tax savings effect would even increase.

♦ **Use fees paid for your child's classes.** If your child is involved in classes and training outside of school, the fees you pay for those classes may be used for the tuition credit. There are certain conditions however, but do not over look this possibility.

♦ **Go to flying school or send your child.** The cost of up to 110 hours of training toward a commercial pilot's license can be used to earn tuition credits.

♦ **Have your employer request that you make a business stop on the way to work.** Travel between your home and work is not considered a business expense; however, if your employer asks you to make a regular stop on the way in to work it is considered a business expense. If the mail or courier is between home and work ask your employer to require you to stop there on the way in to work and make your travel expense deductible.

♦ **Deduct fees paid for advice.** This is often over looked. You are entitled to deduct fees paid for investment and tax planning advice. And if you pay someone to prepare your tax returns that is deductible too.

♦ **Avoid a war — deal with the cottage before you die.** Leaving the family cottage in a will is a recipe for disaster. First, since it's not your principle residence, Revenue Canada will want your estate to pay capital gains tax on the increase in its value. They will treat it as if it was sold on the day you died. A value will be assessed and capital gains tax calculated even if you're passing it on to your children. Then secondly, after your estate has paid the tax, your children may spend years fighting over how and when they can use it. Sit down with them now and work out an agreement, then set up a trust or corporation and transfer the cottage to it. Next give shares in the corporation to your children. Done deal.

♦ **Guaranteed, No-Risk, TAX-FREE, 40% Annual Return.** Here's an absolutely risk-free strategy that's failure proof — PAY OFF YOUR DEBTS! I'm referring here to your non-tax deductible consumer debt. (Get rid of it — It's killing most families today anyway!)

The problem is that you have to pay your debts with the money you have left after paying the taxman. So, if you're in a 50% tax bracket and you have a credit card that you're paying 20% interest on, then just paying it off, is the same as earning a 40% annual return on your investment. To compound the problem, if you are also earning interest income from any of your investments, you're paying 50% of that to the taxman too!

Consumer debt is expensive and it's a trap that ensnares many, silently stealing their dreams and opportunities. Live debt-free, it's profitable.

♦ **Have your investments mature after year-end.** If you're in the practice of purchasing short-term investment such as 6-month term deposits, purchase a 7-month term instead, if it will mean that your investment would have matured in December. By having it mature in January you can defer the reporting of income and paying of tax for one year. Watch the maturity dates and have them mature in your favor, not Revenue Canada's.

♦ **Make a political contribution.** I almost can't believe I'm including this one, with all the problems politicians have created for us all. But, if you have some great inside information about who can get us out of this TAX mess, donate some money to their party.

The tax credit available for putting more food in the political trough is by far the most generous of all credits. The credit is 75% of the first $100 of donation. So, a donation of $100 will only cost you $25.

Good Luck! I hope you put your money on a winner.

Once upon a time, government budgets were balanced, our money was sound, the streets were safe, and taxes imposed by all levels of government took less than 10% of our income.
—Harry Browne (1933-)

❧ Secret 6 ❧
Charitable Giving

Statistics tell us that three quarters of all Canadians do not take advantage of the benefits of charitable giving. Only 25.5% of Canadians who filed tax returns for the 1999 tax year made donations to registered charities. The average donation by percentage was just over half of one percent of their income, an average gift of only $915 Canadian dollars each. By contrast Americans donated 2½ times more than Canadians. The average American charitable donation was $3,441 United States Dollars.

I have explained charitable giving strategies to people who had not been inclined to give before, showing them why they should become givers. People, who were previously inclined to give, become bigger givers! Why?

The Best-Kept Secret of Prosperity

Charitable giving has significant benefits in tax planning. However, giving, and I mean specifically tithing, is also the best-kept secret of prosperity in existence. Tithing is an ancient secret that has been forgotten, ignored and neglected. The principle of tithing has been written and spoken about by many successful people over the ages. Although it is a Biblical principle, people of many diverse beliefs and religions have also used it to their benefit.

What Is Tithing?

Tithing is the systematic, regular giving of one-tenth of all your income back to God. Tithers believe that God is the source of all their prosperity, that He can be trusted to supply all their needs (Philippians 4:19), and that His promises are universal. If you've never tithed before, you need to put it to the test. The following quote from the Biblical book of Malachi, chapter 3, and verse 10 challenges us to test whether God will bless us if we will tithe:

> *"Bring all the tithes into the storehouse so there will be enough food in my temple. If you do," says the Lord Almighty, "I will open the windows of heaven for you. I will pour out a blessing so great you won't have enough room to take it in! Let me prove it to you!"*

Ask people who tithe faithfully and they will tell you of the ten, hundred, and thousand times returns they have received by giving. Universally, tithers will also all tell you that if you tithe you'll

Live Better on the 90%
Than You Ever Did Before on the 100%.

The prosperity benefits of tithing are so significant that it would be worth it even if it came without any tax benefits. However, there are also tax benefits to tithing. Why? Because the government has to encourage giving from the private sector, there are many opportunities to reduce your taxes, while helping needy, religious or social organizations at the same time.

Talk About A Win-Win Situation!

Many people think of charitable giving as leaving a bag of clothing for the Salvation Army at their front door. Yes, this is a form of giving, but certainly only the tip of the iceberg when it comes to using the income tax act to enhance the recipient's and your position.

Charitable donations entitle you to earn tax credits. On your first $200 of donations, for the year, you'll receive a 16% federal tax credit. Because the amount of provincial tax you have to pay is a percentage of the federal tax, this credit is really worth about 26% of your donation in tax credits. The credit reduces your combined federal and provincial taxes by approximately 26% of your donation.

All donations made, during the year, above $200 earn you a 29% federal tax credit. When you add in the effect of the provincial tax, this credit is worth about 50% of your donation. So, after the first $200, for each $1 you donate approximately 50¢ comes right back into your pocket.

There is an annual limit on the amount of charitable donations you can use to earn tax credits. The limit is now 75% of your net annual income. If you give more than Revenue Canada will allow you to use in any year, you can carry the credits forward for up to 5 years.

Since many people give very small donations and may not give regularly, here are a couple ways to increase the benefit of the tax credit if you give less than $1,000 per year:

1. Pool the tax credit with your spouse. Put all your receipts together so that you can qualify for the larger tax credit (over $200), rather than each spouse claiming a smaller amount. Suppose you and you spouse each gave $200 in a year. If each of you claimed the $200 separately, the tax

credit would be worth only $104 (200x26%x2). However, if you pooled the receipts, your tax credit would be worth $152 (200x26% + 200x50%).

2. Save up the receipts. Since you can carry forward the credit for 5 years, consider using the credit in a future year when you've given enough money to qualify for the bigger credit.

There are also additional and creative ways of donating beyond making direct payments to your favorite charity. These strategies require careful planning with the aid of a good financial planner and/or estate planner. Two giving opportunities you may not have considered are:

♦ **Gifts of Life Insurance**
Purchase a life insurance policy on your life and donate it to your charity. Revenue Canada treats the premiums you pay on the policy the same way they treat a direct donation to the charity. After the end of each year you would receive a receipt, for the premiums paid, and all other direct donations you made to your charity during the year. At the time of your death the charity receives the amount that your life was insured for. What an incredible way to multiply your gift!

This strategy is something that should be done as an additional gift and not taken from your current giving to your charity, because they rely on current giving to maintain their ongoing activities.

♦ **Charitable Remainder Trust**
If you've decided to leave part of your estate to a charity, your estate could benefit by significantly

reducing or eliminating any tax liability. However, there may be a better way than leaving it through your will. Instead of having your estate enjoy the tax credit that will result from a donation after your death, you can benefit from the use of the tax credits now while you're still alive, by using a charitable remainder trust.

What is a trust? A simple way to understand what a trust is, is to think of it as a pail. The settlor is the person who puts water (money or other assets) in the pail. The trustee is the person or organization who is responsible for looking after and holding the pail (by something called a trust agreement). The beneficiary is the person or organization who benefits from what's in the pail. Benefits can be received by tapping the pail with a spigot and receiving a small regular portion, ladling out portions as needed (capital encroachment) or pouring out the contents of the pail at some agreed upon time.

A charitable remainder trust is a trust in which you can place any assets you own. Then while you're alive, you get the income that is earned from the assets. And when you die, the charity gets to keep the remaining capital or investment asset.

Revenue Canada views putting your assets in the trust as a gift made to the charity and entitles you to the normal tax credits for charitable donations. However, the value of the tax credit varies depending on the amount and the age of the person establishing the trust. A professional advisor can calculate the benefit that you would receive from establishing one of these trusts.

There are four winners with a charitable remainder trust:

1. The charity gets the right to the assets immediately and never has to be concerned whether you will leave it to them in your will.

2. You get a tax credit. Which can be used immediately or over the next 5 years.

3. You continue to receive income from your assets for the rest of your life just as you would have before setting up the trust.

4. Your estate benefits too. After your death the assets of the trust are paid directly to the charity rather than going through your estate. This saves your estate the cost of probate fees and other costs.

There Are Really 4 Great Reasons To Be A Charitable Giver:

1. It is one of the best ways to take back some control from government. If individuals in society become more proactive and get involved, then we'll need less and less government; not to mention the fact that this way you get to directly decide where your money goes and how it is spent. The more we all do, the less the government will try to take over.

2. Tax benefits. You get the help of having 50¢ of every dollar you give returned to you by way of a tax savings.

3. You'll enjoy the wonderful feeling of supporting organizations and work that is close to you heart. At least it will be after you start giving because wisdom says,

"Wherever your treasure is, there your heart and thoughts will also be."

4. You'll prosper from the universal law of tithing. It is impossible to discuss giving and tithing without examining what the Bible references have to say on the subject. In the book of Luke, chapter 6 and verse 38, Jesus said:

"If you give, you will receive. Your gift will return to you in full measure, pressed down, shaken together to make room for more, and running over. Whatever measure you use in giving—large or small—it will be used to measure what is given back to you."

If You Give, You Will Receive!

Rights are not a privilege conferred by government. They are every human being's entitlement by virtue of his humanity. The right to life does not depend, and must not be contingent, on the pleasure of anyone else, not even a parent or sovereign... You must weep that your government, at present, seems blind to this truth.
—Agnes Gonxha Beiaxhiu, better known as
Mother Teresa (1910-1997)

❧ Secret 7 ❧
Invest Offshore

The conditions of poor government economics, punishing taxation and increasing threats of lawsuits within Canada have created a fierce determination, by Canadians, to reduce taxes and protect their assets by moving money "offshore."

What does the term "offshore investing" mean? It is creating a new entity, such as an offshore international business company (IBC). Then having the company make investments. Some people believe they are investing offshore by buying foreign investments through their onshore-managed investment fund. However, what I mean by the term "offshore investing" is actually creating a new entity offshore.

The term "offshore" conjures up many different images. Offshore ventures are sometimes viewed as risky investments. However, in reality, offshore investing is simply creating a structure or entity in another country for the purpose of investing. The investments can be as simple as opening an interest bearing bank account or as risky as stock speculation and/or commodity trading.

Offshore Investing is a financial trend spreading like a raging wild fire. The Vancouver Sun newspaper called it a "...*sizzling hot topic for boomers.*" MacLean's magazine labeled it as "...*tapping into a fierce determination among many middle-and-upper-income Canadians to reduce their taxes and protect their assets.*"

Due to the fact that Canada doesn't have exchange controls (restriction of currency crossing borders), no one knows for sure how much money leaves Canada each year. However, economist Tom Naylor of McGill University in Montreal, an expert on international flight capital and author of the 1994 book, **Hot Money and the Politics of Debt,** estimates that tens of billions of dollars leaves Canada each year, headed for offshore jurisdictions.

It is estimated that one-third of the world's wealth (over $5 trillion) is managed or held in one or more of the 45 or so offshore financial centers. The world's largest banks are all involved — Barclays Bank's (11th largest bank in the world) most profitable branch is in the offshore jurisdiction of Jersey, Channel Islands. The Canadian Imperial Bank of Commerce (CIBC) earned most of its last year's $1.69 billion profit in its low-tax Caribbean operations, which allowed it to pay only $51 million of tax for the year. That's only 3%! Imagine if you only had to pay 3% income tax last year. Furthermore, it is reputed that Cayman Islands alone handles more deposits than any other country, except USA and Japan. And, there are 418 bank and trust companies licensed to do business in the Bahamas, whereas Canada has only 84.

For years, the world's wealthiest families and individuals have used offshore strategies to achieve powerful benefits in estate, business succession, investment, asset protection and tax planning. Offshore investing can cut investment income tax to zero and it's the absolute best estate-planning tool in the world. It keeps your money away from creditors, lawyers, ex-spouses and anyone else who would like to get their hands on it.

Investing offshore and becoming a tax exile is easy. If you can open up a bank account, you can invest offshore. The popularity of going offshore and the ease with which we now communicate and do business globally, has really expanded this opportunity. Once the exclusive domain of the super-rich – it used to cost a fortune just in legal fees – offshore investing in our global economy is now available to people with as little as $10,000 or more to invest.

Why Go Offshore?

Everyone has his or her own specific motives for going offshore. However, I believe that the only time to make any significant change, such as going offshore, is when doing nothing becomes a greater risk and/or cost than making the change. Therefore, I like to examine the question, "Why go offshore?" in terms of the problems onshore, that make it necessary to go offshore.

As humans we all go through much the same process in solving problems. As you read this today you will be at one of the following 4 steps to solving the problems that I will identify in this chapter:

1. We all start off in various states of unconsciousness, oblivious to the fact that the problems even exist. *None are more hopelessly enslaved than those who falsely believe they are free. — Johann Wolfgang von Goethe*

2. The first real step to solving the problems comes when we become conscious of the problem's existence and its current, or future potential, negative effect on our lives.

3. The next step is to find workable realistic solutions to the problem.

4. And finally, become sufficiently motivated to take

positive steps to solve the problem using the information gained in step 3.

In my opinion, we must go offshore because of the immensity of the following five problems that exist onshore. All other reasons for going offshore will be part of these five. *You only need to be affected by one of these five problems to take action!*

The FIVE problems:
1. Punitive taxes
2. Attacks on our assets through epidemic spurious litigation and unwarranted illegal government seizures
3. Government intervention in our lives and businesses
4. No privacy
5. Low rates of return on investment.

Are you affected by any of these problems?

I will discuss and explain how going offshore solves these problems, under the following four headings:

1. The Ultimate Tax Shelter — LOW, or NO TAXES
2. Privacy
3. Asset Protection
4. High Profit Potential

The Ultimate Tax Shelter

The next big tax-grab already underway is estate taxes. Personally, I find it totally out of integrity that when an individual accumulates wealth – no matter how large or small – it has already been taxed. (Literally – to death – in this case). Yet when you or I want to leave our hard-earned money to our heirs, the government, in their waste and sloth, feels the need to tax it again!

Offshore investing is the best estate-planning tool in the entire world. No probate. No legal fees. No estate taxes. Nothing. You just pass the access on to your children without any consequences whatsoever. The reason for this is that the offshore assets are not in your name and therefore can never become part of your estate. At the time of your death access is passed on to whomever you have appointed. Your trustee or director (depending what type of structure you've set up) will continue to manage the assets as before; however, now for the benefit of your heirs.

Eliminate Income Tax On Your Investment Returns

In regard to income taxes, accounts resident in offshore financial centers are not taxed at source nor do the financial institutions report any income to authorities. Furthermore, offshore financial centers such as Bahamas, Belize, Grand Cayman and the Channel Islands have **NO INCOME TAX** whatsoever. There are approximately 45 countries that do not have an income tax, capital gains tax, or estate tax! Other offshore financial centers, such as Panama and Costa Rica that do have an income tax, have either written legislation making their international business companies exempt from tax or they allow these companies to earn income **TAX-FREE** if it is earned outside of their country.

Therefore, let's say you have $100,000 invested in Canada and your investment is earning 10% per year (you wish). And, if you're in a 50% income tax bracket, then over then next 10 years, your $100,000 compounded annually becomes $162,889. Your net rate of return is only 5%.

On the other hand, if the same $100,000 was invested offshore at a 10% rate of return and a 0% tax rate it would be worth $259,374 at the end of 10 years, an increase of 59%. Stated more emphatically, paying no tax would increase your yield 2½ times, and put an extra $96,485 in your pocket at the **same rate of return!**

Privacy

Privacy is a right. Do you believe that? Unfortunately, the majority of people today believe that the only people who need privacy are people that are doing something illegal, have something to hide, or the government! Well, I disagree with that. I believe that PRIVACY is your RIGHT! You should have the right to do business with whomever you want to do business, without anybody interfering. As long as you are not infringing on anybody else's same right or breaking some laws. The right to privacy in all of your affairs should be your protected right!

However, since the majority of Canadians don't believe that privacy should be a right, they vote to allow their government to pass more and more legislation giving it ever-increasing powers to invade our privacy. New anti-terrorist legislation will now further erode personal privacy onshore. Police organizations around the world are telling their citizens that privacy is an "ANTISOCIAL ACT". This means the rest of us have to work that much harder to preserve our privacy.

Furthermore, one of our greatest business and communication assets is helping erode our privacy — the computer. We are all leaving an electronic trail. I love computers, but as faster and faster computers are being developed, tying together more and more databases every day, you have a greater chance of having your privacy violated. It's getting easier and easier to access that data. And there's now more of it than ever before. It is believed that there are approximately 25 active files on the average person, while those who have a higher profile may have as many as 200. **Who's looking over your shoulder?**

Onshore banks are not protecting our privacy either. I have to tell you a story. I made a branch-to-branch deposit in Saskatchewan at a Canadian chartered bank. I was depositing money into a friend's account in British Columbia. Following the transaction, the teller passed me the deposit receipt. Fine, I expected that. But on the receipt was my friend's current balance in that account. That's scary. This is onshore banking!

This Is Onshore Privacy! — NO Privacy.

This kind of thing doesn't happen in offshore banking centers around the world — because it's against the law. Laws onshore are written to invade privacy rather than protect it. Almost every country now has a bank privacy or bank secrecy act. It is misnamed, because the act doesn't protect privacy, rather it lays out the conditions, rights and powers to break the privacy without your knowledge or permission, free of liability. When you apply for a bank account onshore your signature releases the bank of any liability in releasing information on your accounts. There is no law that says a bank teller or bank manager cannot disclose information on any client or any client's business activities to Revenue Canada.

Onshore banks also sell your name and personal information to marketing companies. And, if an employee of Revenue Canada walks into your bank (even without proper identification) and asks them for your information, they bend over backwards to get it for them, while you wait in long lines for service. Offshore banks take pride in protecting your privacy. There are cases where they've had IRS agents arrested for illegally attempting to gain information at world-banking centers offshore.

Asset Protection

The insurance industry talks often about the whole aspect of buying creditor proof investments. And they're not wrong. Creditor proof investments are assets that cannot be attached in the event of a bankruptcy or a liability situation. In Canada, life insurance assets are protected. But, as good as that is, they are still visible, and creditors still know they are there. Eventually you're going to need to use your funds and when you go to take them your creditors are going to have access to the income stream.

On the other hand, you can go offshore and your creditors then have to first of all come after your assets in the offshore jurisdiction. This is very hard to do, and even harder to know if, or where, you have any money. PLUS, if your assets aren't in your name, they can't attach them anyway. If the assets are in an account owned by an international business company (IBC), they are not **your** personal assets. Your creditors can sue you but they can't get the assets because legally they don't belong to you, they belong to the offshore company.

With your assets offshore you have the best asset protection in the world: protection from creditors, business partners,

88

governments, and even in spouse-to-spouse situations.

You may look at your affairs today and conclude that you're not likely to get sued, but let me ask you 5 questions:
1. What would happen to what you own if you were sued?
2. Would you or could you lose it all?
3. How much sense does it make to work your whole life and then see it all disappear because you didn't plan?
4. Statistically over the next year your chance of having a house fire is 1 in 244 while your chance of being sued could be as high as 1 in 5!
5. A house fire is extremely rare — Do you own fire insurance? Why?

How could it happen to you? Maybe you could be sued due to: a car accident, recreational accident, accidents of all kinds, business failure, business partner disagreement, marriage breakdown, etc. No one can see into the future. No one likes to think about disasters. But let's be realistic, these things do happen. If they didn't there wouldn't be so many lawyers.

Don't let these legal vultures have what is rightfully yours. Hide your assets so that nobody can find them, and even if they could, they couldn't get their hands on them. A properly formed offshore structure can provide you a level of asset protection and privacy equaled only to being invisible.

High Profit Potential
Personal experience has taught me that nobody goes offshore for less than 10%. Yet droves of people go to onshore banks for 3-5%. Anywhere you go around the world you can find investments that earn 10% — and better — consistently year after year.

In 1999 the top 350 offshore investment funds had an annual return of over 91%! Of the 350 funds, 279 of them returned 100% or more. How would you like to double your money in one year? And if that's not good enough, the top two funds earned over 1,000%. Although 1999 was an exceptional year, some of the top 350 offshore investment funds have achieved 5-year returns of between 800% and 900%. Standard & Poor's provides information on offshore investment funds through their website and printed publications. You can access their information online at **www.funds-sp.com** . You may be amazed to learn that many specialty funds earn 3 digit annual returns.

For those who don't want to make their own investment decisions, there are also many very well respected asset management companies and investment banks that will manage your portfolio for you. Provided your portfolio meets their minimum size requirement.

Take Control of Your Finances – TODAY! Diversify By Going Offshore.

When you combine the tax savings with the high profit potential, offshore investing cannot be ignored. You've heard over and over that diversification is one of the priorities of investing. True diversification means offshore investing.

Any investing has risks, which must be taken into consideration. However, offshore investing, done sensibly, and structured properly can be safer than buying certificates of deposit from your local bank. For example, no Swiss bank, chartered to do banking under the laws of Switzerland, and incorporated in Switzerland, has gone broke in over 200 years. As a matter of fact, no Swiss bank has gone bankrupt in modern times. There are many good financial institutions offshore that you can work with. For your reference, as of May 1, 2002, Canada's largest bank ranks only number 44 by assets, according to the Bankers Almanac list of top world banks.

Although new government regulations are constantly being written and implemented regarding offshore investing, the benefits of asset protection, privacy, tax advantages and profit potential, still make offshore investing a very attractive option. I encourage you to go offshore now before your government tries to make it illegal.

Some would say that although these offshore strategies satisfy the letter of the law, they go against the spirit of the law. Ask yourself - Which is more corrupt: Canadian senators charging the government of Canada $2.8 million per year for airplane tickets, rather than utilizing their expense accounts, which you'd assume were set up for this very purpose? Or, the efforts of every citizen to deny the government as much money as legally possible so as to force it back on the road of financial responsibility and to protect what they have worked so hard to earn?

Set up *properly*, offshore investment structures satisfy the letter of the law and are very effective ways of protecting investment assets and allowing individuals to operate their affairs in complete *privacy*. Something impossible to do in Canada.

Even conservative accountants agree. In Deloitte & Touche's annual tax planning book, *How To Reduce The Tax You Pay*, they say, ***"Investing offshore is still an attractive***

option for many Canadians, *but you should be aware of the risks involved, both at home in terms of increased tax vigilance and abroad because of inherent risks. Consult a professional investment advisor before taking your money outside Canada."*

If you would like to learn more about going offshore I would be please to speak with you or refer you to someone who can assist you. You may contact me through my publisher or by E-mail at **david@davidvoth.com**

Dear Revenue Canada,

I am writing to you to cancel my subscription. Please remove my name from your mailing list.

Thanks,
Dave

How Would You Like To Stop Paying Income Tax Completely?

One of the ways to become a **TAX-FREE** citizen is to become a non-resident of Canada. You see the government of Canada taxes its residents not its citizens. You can keep your citizenship; just become a non-resident for tax purposes. Depending on your situation and your attitude about maintaining your Canadian residency, you may be able to become a tax exile of Canada. Once you've completed the strategy you will no longer have to pay any more income tax.

How do you become recognized as a non-resident? Obviously if you pack up all that you have and move to another country you are a non-resident. That would make sense to most people, right? Well, apparently not to the bureaucrats at Revenue Canada. They decided that they should come up with a test to determine whether in fact you are a non-resident.

In addition to the Income Tax Act, Revenue Canada writes thousands of Interpretation Bulletins to help explain sections of the Act. It is important to note that these bulletins do not have the force of law. However, they can be helpful in determining how Revenue Canada may respond in various situations. One such bulletin is called IT-221R3, 'Determination of an Individual's Residency Status'. You can get your own copy by visiting their website. If you'd rather not surf their whole site, you can go directly to the bulletin by using this link: **http://www.ccra-adrc.gc.ca/E/pub/tp/it22r3eq/it221 r3-e.html**

In Revenue Canada's own words, this is what they say is the purpose of the bulletin:

The purpose of this bulletin is to explain the position of the Canada Customs and Revenue Agency (CCRA) concerning the determination of an individual's residence status for income tax purposes and the factors to be taken into account in making that determination.

In Revenue Canada's opinion you will be considered a non-resident if you meet certain criteria. The primary test is whether you have resident ties with Canada. These are: Do you have a) a dwelling place, b) spouse or common-law spouse who will be staying behind, and c) dependents, in Canada.

Elements of a secondary test, which may be used to determine residency, include:

a. Personal property in Canada (such as furniture, clothing, automobiles and recreational vehicles),

b. Social ties with Canada (such as memberships in Canadian recreational and religious organizations),

c. Economic ties with Canada (such as employment with a Canadian employer and active involvement in a Canadian business, and Canadian bank accounts, retirement savings plans, credit cards, and securities accounts),

d. Landed immigrant status or appropriate work permits in Canada,

e. Hospitalization and medical insurance coverage from a province or territory of Canada,

f. Driver's license from a province or territory of Canada,

g. Vehicle registered in a province or territory of Canada,

h. Seasonal dwelling place in Canada or a leased dwelling place referred to in, and

i. Memberships in Canadian unions or professional organizations.

As you go through this list, if you feel that Revenue Canada would still consider you to be a resident, don't worry, now you know what they're looking for and you can change you're current situation to become a non-resident. For example, you could place property in a trust to get it out of your name.

As a non-resident for tax purposes, you can still live (visit) in Canada. And, as long as you spend no more than 182 days per year in Canada you will never regain your "tax residency."

This presents a considerable opportunity for retirees who live in Canada in summer and live in the warm south in the winter. Many retirees already spend less than 182 days per year in Canada. So, if they just satisfy the other requirements, they could...

Stop Paying Income Taxes Completely.

If this strategy interests you, I recommend a good book on the subject. It is entitled; *Take Your Money And Run!* first published in July 1994 and republished as a revised and updated edition in 2001, written by former Bay Street financial analyst Alex Doulis. The paperback has become one of the best-selling business books in Canadian history. The book, written in a story format, tells how its central character planned his escape, implemented his strategies, and now lives **TAX-FREE** beyond the reach of Revenue Canada.

Here's an Idea!

Many people fear being "downsized" or forced to retire. Look at it from a new perspective. Take the early retirement package now. Put your retiring allowance into an RRSP

TAX-FREE. Move to your favorite offshore destination. You can then use your registered funds as needed, only paying the withholding tax (maximum 25%, 10% on withdrawals of up to $5,000). Start a consulting business to other businesses, or market information, around the world by computer. The ease with which we can now communicate and do business internationally allows you to live anywhere you like. It is no longer necessary for you to be living in close proximity to your clients. You can move to a beautiful part of the world and live there **TAX-FREE.** Enjoy a fantastic lifestyle where you can live like a millionaire for less than $20,000 per year!

A piece of freedom is no longer enough for human beings. . . unlike bread, a slice of liberty does not finish hunger. Freedom is like life. It cannot be had in installments. Freedom is indivisible - we have it all, or we are not free.
—Martin Luther King, Jr. (1929-1968)

If every man has freedom to do all that he wills, provided he infringes not the equal freedom of any other man, then he is free to drop connection with the State—to relinquish its protection, and to refuse paying toward its support.

—Herbert Spencer, philosopher (1820-1903)

⤳ Secret 8 ⤳
Buy An
Insurance Tax Shelter

The life insurance industry is a tax haven, and will likely always enjoy that status, because of all the special laws created just for it. You can spend time wondering why, or you can use their heavily favored status to your advantage!

One popular strategy is the Life Insurance Tax Shelter. Over the last 15 years Canadians have stuffed millions and millions of dollars into these programs. The reason is that they allow either tax-deferred or **TAX-FREE** treatment of your investment dollars, with no risk. It's the best onshore tax avoidance investment strategy available!

What Is An Insurance Tax Shelter?

An Insurance Tax Shelter is a plan issued by a life insurance company that allows you to deposit any amount of money and shelter all of the growth of the investment from income tax. Each insurance company gives their plan its own unique name.

How Does It Work?

Revenue Canada allows insurance companies to issue these plans and maintain their tax-sheltered status as long as they satisfy certain conditions. These plans are considered "exempt" by Revenue Canada under sections 12.2 and 148 of the Income Tax Act. The insurance company must maintain a minimum amount of life insurance on each plan to keep it tax exempt. This insurance however, can and should be low cost decreasing coverage, only enough to keep the plan tax exempt. The amount of life insurance necessary is based on a Revenue Canada formula and each plan must meet an annual test.

What Makes The Strategy Work?

Why do these plans out perform other non-sheltered investments?

♦ *First,* Your earnings build-up **TAX-FREE** within the plan

♦ And *second,* the annual expense charges of the plan cost less than the tax, which would have to be paid on the annual investment earnings of a similar non-sheltered investment.

EXAMPLE: Assuming a 10% annual rate of return. A couple, both age 45, in a 50% tax bracket would have to pay a total of $43,244 of income tax on the earnings of an investment of $10,000 per year over 10 years.

By contrast, if they invested $10,000 per year for 10 years into a tax-sheltered insurance account, earning the same rate of return; they would pay only $10,701 in total expense charges to the insurance company over the 10 years.

These plans are flexible, allowing you to vary the amount of your deposits and choose the type of investments, from GICs to investment fund indexes, with no restriction on foreign content.

How Do You Get Your Money Out?

When it comes time to take income, you can generate income from your plan one of two ways:

1. You can make direct withdrawals, **TAX-FREE** from the tax-sheltered account, up to the adjusted cost base (ACB) of the plan without incurring any tax. Simply stated, the ACB is equal to your deposits less the cost of insurance. Once you have withdrawn the **TAX-FREE** portion of the account, Revenue Canada will consider any further withdrawals to be taxable. Your insurance company can tell you what the ACB is for your account so that you don't withdraw more than you want to.

2. Under a special arrangement, you can leverage your account with a bank. This is the real benefit of an Insurance Tax Shelter! The leveraging of your account is what allows the plan to outperform other investment vehicles, because a loan is never taxable!

   How Is It Structured? When it comes time to take income from your plan, the bank will accept your plan as security for a loan. You can then make a single loan or a series of annual loans that you will use as income. The bank will capitalize the loan payments, so that you never have to make payments on the loan. Because the tax-sheltered growth within the plan continues to grow **TAX-FREE** the bank has an ever-increasing asset with which to secure each year's loan. The loan is eventually repaid from the **TAX-FREE** insurance payout, when you die. And then, the insurance payout in excess of the bank loan balance is paid out **TAX-FREE** to your beneficiaries. Since a loan is not taxable, this plan allows you to **Earn All Of Your Income TAX-FREE!**

BONUS – If you die before you can spend or withdraw all of the money in your plan, the balance of the tax-sheltered account, plus the insurance amount, is paid **TAX-FREE** to your beneficiaries. And, insurance payouts avoid probate.

The following is an example illustration supplied to me by a certified financial planner who represents one of the 35 insurance companies that offer Insurance Tax Shelters. Don't get hung up by the numbers, because every illustration is unique, relative to variables such as age, gender, smoking status, interest rates, etc. The purpose of this example is just to show the effect of the **TAX-FREE** income that can be generated from these plans. Your financial planner can generate a personalized illustration for you:

> **EXAMPLE:** This illustration assumes you deposit $13,500 annually into the plan for 18 years and then start to take a **TAX-FREE** bank loan starting in the 24th year. The lending institution would extend annual **TAX-FREE** loans to you of $78,905 adjusted annually for a 2% cost of living adjustment for the next 31 years.

By contrast, if you attempted the same thing with an RRSP, depositing $13,500 for 18 years and then took the same level of after-tax income starting in the 24th year, you would exhaust your RRSP in as little as 9 years. That's the impact of **TAX-FREE** income in retirement. Plus with the Insurance Tax Shelter, since you had no taxable income, you still qualify for the maximum Old Age Security payments.

Now if we examine what would happen if we used a non tax-sheltered investment, the effect is even more staggering. Using the exact same assumptions of:

deposits, rate of return and income at retirement, a fully taxed investment would be exhausted in slightly less than 5 years. That's because it does not enjoy the tax-sheltered growth of either an Insurance Tax Shelter or an RRSP.

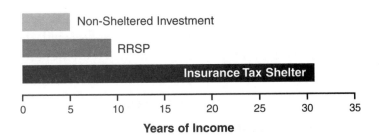

Another observation of the Insurance Tax Shelter reveals what happens if you don't live until retirement. Suppose you died after 10 years of making deposits. The Insurance Tax Shelter would provide $1,000,000 **TAX-FREE** to your beneficiaries. While the RRSP would only be worth approximately $200,000, but Revenue Canada would grab half of it, leaving your family a **TAX-FREE** equivalent of only $100,000!

10 Times More For Your Family!

Look at it this way – 20 years from now, you're either dead or alive. If you're alive, no other plan will pay you more after tax income. And if you're dead, no other plan will pay more money to your family – and do it **TAX-FREE!**

Retirement Income Strategy — When you start to use your assets to fund your retirement income, use the funds from your least tax efficient investments first. As we saw from the example a non-registered investment can only provide income about half as long as an RRSP and an RRSP less than a third as long as an Insurance Tax Shelter. Therefore, it is prudent to use funds from your non-registered (non-sheltered) investments first, then your RRSP assets and finally tap your Insurance Tax Shelter. This strategy will give you the best bang-for-the-buck while you're alive! And after you die, all the value left in your Insurance Tax Shelter will be paid out **TAX-FREE** directly to your named beneficiaries, avoiding your estate and probate tax.

Who Else Says So?

Besides the insurance industry and me writing this book telling you how great these plans are at exploiting the tax laws, it's always good to know if there are other credible recommendations from other professionals. Accountants are recommending these plans to their clients. This is what they are saying:

> *"Tax-sheltered insurance accounts are an excellent way of building assets for retirement. At retirement, borrowing tax-free income is a strategy that will maximize spendable income while avoiding benefit clawbacks and reducing or eliminating tax payable."*
> **Terry Laughren,** Chartered Accountant

> *"Individuals looking for tax shelters or deferral mechanisms may wish to explore the benefits that may be derived from an "exempt" life insurance policy. Such policies may be a powerful tool in the tax planning arsenal, particularly when many other tax shelters appear to have been curtailed."*

"The returns from virtually tax-free accumulation after the deduction of the insurance costs, compared to taxable accumulations, can, over a long period, be quite remarkable."

Tax Planning Checklist,
PriceWaterhouseCoopers

"The life insurance industry has developed attractive and highly sophisticated products that can help you meet two planning objectives at once: having insurance coverage, and providing retirement income from tax-sheltered growth. These policies allow you to pay insurance premiums and make deposits to a tax-sheltered investment account at the same time. Professional advice is a must when assessing the merits of this type of investment."

Tax Planning for You and Your Family,
KPMG Accountants

"The past decade has seen tremendous change in the financial services sector — regulatory change has resulted in new competitors and a proliferation of unique and sophisticated products and services. The insurance industry, once considered a sleepy backwater in the financial community, has recognized the need to change in order to survive and is now on the forefront on many new developments in products and services."

The Canadian Guide to Wealth Preservation and Accumulation,
Canadian Institute of Chartered Accountants

I recommend these plans to wide age range of people. From young people in their early 20's, starting their first investment plan; to seniors in their late 60's, looking for ways to shelter money in retirement. It's hard to find situations where these tax-sheltered insurance accounts aren't superior to other types of comparable investments.

Not all products offered by insurance companies are the same, and you should make sure the financial planner who you're dealing with works with sound institutions. However, assuming that is the case, you will be amazed at how much extra money you could end up with, down the road, and by not paying taxes as you go! Life insurance tax-sheltered investments have very unique positions in the tax laws, and should be investigated at every opportunity.

Let's review the features and benefits of owning an Insurance Tax Shelter:

♦ Deposit flexibility – You can change both the frequency and amount of your deposits

♦ **TAX-FREE** build-up of earnings within the plan

♦ **TAX-FREE** income through an innovative loan program when required

♦ **TAX-FREE** money to heirs upon death

♦ Creditor proof – money in the plan can never be seized by creditors

♦ Complete choice of investments with no restriction on foreign content

♦ Assets in the plan can be used as collateral

♦ No mandatory or minimum income payments in

retirement – If you don't need the income you can continue sheltering the growth within the plan

♦ Since income from the plan is not included in taxable income, the plan could prevent clawbacks on Old Age Security payments or other benefits

An Insurance Tax Shelter is truly a Win-Win-Win plan. Your investment stays **TAX-FREE** while it is building up within the plan. You will earn **TAX-FREE** income from the plan in retirement. And when you're gone, the rest of the money goes to your heirs **TAX-FREE!** Revenue Canada never sees one red cent in this strategy. In my books that's **WINNING!**

You cannot bring about prosperity by discouraging thrift. You cannot strengthen the weak by weakening the strong. You cannot help the wage earner by pulling down the wage payer. You cannot further the brotherhood of man encouraging class hatred. You cannot help the poor by destroying the rich. You cannot keep out of trouble by spending more than you earn. You cannot build character and courage by taking away man's initiative and independence. You cannot help men permanently by doing for them what they could and should do for themselves.
—Abraham Lincoln (1809-1865)

❦ Secret 9 ❧
Start Or Properly Utilize A Small Business

A small business is almost certainly the best tax shelter ever! The tax savings that can be realized from a small business are remarkable. I am not talking about some big enterprise, although that's fine too. Even a simple, sole proprietorship, home-based business could save you thousands of dollars per year that are now being taken from you each month and sent to Revenue Canada.

Don't already own a business? — No problem — now may be the best time in history to start your own business. The depth and volume of resources available today is amazing.

If you now have a job where you have a lot of independence from your employer, you may be able to change your relationship so that you become an independent consultant or contractor rather than an employee. You will then enjoy all of the tax advantages of any other small business!

In fact being prepared to create your own job is the key to finding and keeping employment. Experts tell us that in the United States as much as 40% of the workforce is now on contract and it's increasing. This trend is on the rise in Canada too. Don't fear it—embrace it—because it comes with great opportunities to get control and restructure your situation to reduce tax.

Significant Tax Savings

The tax saving benefits of full or part-time self-employment are very significant. The most significant benefit is all the increased deductions you will be entitled to write off. If you have a home-based business for example, a portion of all of your expenses can now be used as deductions. Things such as: interest, rent, property tax, insurance, utilities, maintenance, Internet access, etc., can now be written off. You have to pay these expenses anyway, setup your own business and you won't have to pay them with after-tax dollars anymore!

In addition you will be able to write off start-up costs, meals and entertainment, travel, education, and automobile expenses. You will also be able to claim deductions for depreciation on things used for your business such as a computer, printer, fax machine, office furniture, or specialized equipment.

Properly utilizing a small business is also the easiest way to split income with your family. You can pay your spouse and children for work they do in the business, which will lower your taxable income. Since there is no tax charged on incomes of less than $7,400, you could pay 2 children and your spouse $7,400 each for work they did in your family business. This would give you $22,200 of salaries to write off as deductions. That's $22,200 **TAX-FREE** that your family could not have enjoyed if you earned the same income at a job!

If you decide to start an enterprise out of your home you won't be alone. Once considered to be unfashionable, working out of a home-based business is now considered chic. Approximately 2.5 million Canadians now own home-based businesses. Just think about it: no boss, no commuting, no getting up in the dark of winter and venturing out at minus 30 degrees (we are in Canada of course), no having to get dressed up to go to work (sweats and t-shirt if you like), no office politics and gossip to make you negative. And think about how much more time you could spend with your family!

When starting a new business it is important to consider what the best business structure is for your venture. There are basically three main types of business structures. Each has its own unique advantages and disadvantages. I will briefly explain each structure and its tax advantage.

Sole Proprietor

This is the simplest type of business. A sole proprietor is fully responsible for all debts and obligations of the business. If you choose to carry on a business under a name other than your own, the government insists that you register with your province. However, if you create a business in your own name, it is not necessary to register it.

The tax advantage of this type of structure is that all the expenses of the business are your own and they can be used as deductions to reduce your taxable income. Many businesses start this way until they become profitable giving the entrepreneur the greatest tax advantage.

Partnership

A partnership is a business owned by two or more persons who have combined their skills and resources. An agreement is drawn up to establish the terms of the business and to protect the partners in the event of a disagreement or wind-up of the business. Partners share in the profits and liabilities of the business according to the terms of their agreement.

The tax treatment of a partnership is similar to that of a sole proprietorship structure. Each partner is responsible for his or her portion of the profit and expenses.

Corporation

A corporation is a legal entity that has a separate legal existence from its owners. Owners of a corporation are called shareholders. Corporations, because they are separate legal entities, are responsible for their own profit and liabilities. Therefore, no shareholder of a corporation is personally liable for the debts or liabilities of the corporation.

The tax advantage of a corporation is that once your business starts to earn a significant amount of profit it can benefit from the lower small business income tax rates. On qualified small business corporation income up to $200,000 per year, the tax rate could be as low as 17.1%; depending on which province the corporation is registered. Then as the shareholder of the corporation, you can pay yourself a dividend, which could allow you to earn up to $28,000 **TAX-FREE** each year; again depending on your province of residency. Higher dividend payments could be earned at low tax rates.

Some tax advisors suggest that it is not a good idea to earn all of your income by way of dividend income because dividend income is not included in Revenue Canada's definition of earned income. Therefore, you would have a lower RRSP contribution limit and it may have the effect of reducing your Canada Pension Plan payments in the future. However, the up side is lower taxes now, and if you utilize other retirement investment vehicles such as the Insurance Tax Shelter and offshore strategies, then you may want to earn all of the income from your small business as dividends. If you and your spouse are both shareholders you could both earn your income from dividends and pay very little or **no personal income tax!**

Starting Up

Need help or ideas in starting up your new business? The business section of your favorite bookstore is full of many useful titles on the subject. There are numerous magazines to browse. And the Internet has hundreds of helpful sites to give you ideas and help you get setup properly. The following are a few sites to help you get started. From there you can click on other links or just type "small business startup" into a search engine and see what comes up. The last time I did it, the search engine told me there were 366,000 results! Adding the word "Canada" cut the results down to "only" 49,300.

Useful business websites:
♦ **Canada Service Business Centres** – Business start-up assistant. This website has information on topics such as investigating your market, structuring, financing and writing a business plan, as well as links to many other sites. **www.bsa.cbsc.org**
♦ **Entrepreneur Magazine's website** – This website has a lot of useful information and links to almost anything you can imagine on business information. **www.entrepreneur.com**
♦ **Inc. Magazine's website** – This website has advice about getting started, writing a business plan, starting a business, running a one-person business, buying a business or franchise; to topics on growing your business such as: customer service, e-commerce, finance & capital, going global, human resources, sales, etc. **www.inc.com**

♦ **Microsoft bCentral Canada** – This website provides online subscription services to help small businesses get online, improve marketing effectiveness, increase sales, and provide better customer service. **www.bcentral.ca**
♦ **Startup Internet Marketing** – Free Tools, Tips, E-books, Training and Startup Strategies. This website has cutting-edge marketing tools and tactics to help grow your business successfully... while saving you time and money! And ninety-five percent of the resources provided here are free.
www.startupinternetmarketing.com

The Internet offers literally thousands of ideas and opportunities for new businesses. The information industry has and continues to be exploding. Global Internet commerce in 1998 was estimated to be $81 billion US dollars. It is expected that the Global Internet commerce in 2003 will be $3.2 Trillion US dollars. Industry Canada expects that the Canadian Internet commerce by 2003 will be $70 billion US dollars, or about 2.1% of the global value. Set up your own Internet business now and you can get a piece of this booming market place!

A great business you may want to get involved in is the information or "knowledge for profit" business. The information business generates billions of dollars through the sale of books, manuals, tapes (video and cassette), and complete courses; I have met people who are earning high six digit incomes in this industry. And now it's possible to do it all over the Internet. For those who can write and publish marketable material that others are interested in buying, this opportunity is literally fantastic. You can live anywhere you'd like to live in the world, work when you want to, and make a good living selling information.

How About Starting A Bed And Breakfast?

From a tax planning perspective, one of the best home-based businesses you can start and operate is a Bed and Breakfast. A bed and breakfast is the ultimate "home" business because your home really becomes your business. As a way of generating tax-deductible expenses, no other home-based business is more effective.

First, your entire home, except your family bedrooms, can legitimately be allocated as space used for your business. And second, since you have to serve meals to your guests, you are allowed to deduct food costs as well as all the other home operating expenses. You must have the gift of hospitality and enjoy entertaining, but if this describes you, jump in with both feet.

The following are a couple of useful websites offering more information about the bed and breakfast industry. More are also available through links you'll find on these sites.

Useful bed and breakfast websites:
♦ **Bed and Breakfast Expo** – This website is dedicated to showcasing Canada's bed and breakfast homes and inns. All of their listings have color photographs and lots of description of the accommodations. The site also has a section on starting your own B & B, offering information, seminars, and books. **www.bbexpo.com**
♦ **International Bed and Breakfast Pages** – This website lists inns with the purpose of increasing the accommodation's visibility on the Internet. It also has sections for innkeepers providing information on: recipes, travel articles, a quarterly newsletter, and

actively promotes Bed & Breakfasts for sale. **www.ibbp.com**

Of course nothing lasts forever and when you go to sell your business, if it is a qualified small business corporation, Revenue Canada allows you to claim a $500,000 **TAX-FREE** capital gains exemption. You can even double this benefit. If you own the business with your spouse you can both claim the exemption and

Earn $1,000,000 TAX-FREE!

Whether you own a business, can change your employment situation to become a business, or you start a sideline, part time, full time or home-based business, **you can enjoy all of the tax benefits allowed for businesses!**

Supreme Court of Canada Ruling

The Supreme Court of Canada is on your side. Back in 1978 the Supreme Court made a ruling that Revenue Canada has been abusing for 24 years. The ruling dealt with a situation in which a taxpayer's expenses were disallowed because it was decided that the taxpayer had no "reasonable-expectation-of-profit". Over the last 24 years Revenue Canada has been using this ruling to take advantage of entrepreneurs.

Well, all that changed on May 23, 2002. You will recall that I wrote about this Supreme Court ruling in Secret 4, referring to investment losses. It is a very important ruling and that's why I am highlighting it here again. Remember, from now on Revenue Canada can only test whether an investment or expense is related to a hobby, personal activity or personal use. The ruling clearly says, "Where the nature of an activity is clearly commercial, there is no need to analyze the taxpayer's business decisions". The Court added, that the test "should not be used to second-guess the business judgment of the taxpayer. It is the commercial nature of the taxpayer's activity which must be evaluated not his or her business acumen".

This is an extremely good decision in favor of all the entrepreneurs of Canada. Investment into many high-risk ventures may previously have been disallowed by Revenue Canada because of the so-called "reasonable-expectation-of-profit" test. Let's put that in perspective, this judgment-call was coming from a public servant who never took a risk in his or her life. Entrepreneurs on the other hand thrive on the hope and excitement of creating something great and making a profit. The very nature of stepping out on your own to create something has many inherent risks. Now at least if things don't work out the way you expect, you can write off the losses without fear of punishment from Revenue Canada.

Current Business Owners Beware: You May Be Overpaying Your Taxes

If you already have a business you may still be over paying your taxes. Why? Well, most business tax preparers are used to

answering your questions, instead of telling you what you should be asking. They are trained to take your information and file returns with it, using the best options available at filing time to reduce your tax as much as possible.

However, the real opportunity lies in forward planning

and unfortunately many accountants do not have the time, nor take the time, to do this type of strategic planning with their small business clients. And let's face it; you as a business owner want to concentrate on doing business. It's always too easy to think that your accountant is looking after these things for you. But unfortunately that thought may be costing you a lot now and maybe even a lot more in the years to come. That's why it's very important to set aside some time now and uncover all of the possible ways to reduce the tax you pay. Set up a meeting with your tax advisor financial planner today!

Don't Delay — Do It Today!

Whatever
The Mind of Man
Can
Conceive
And
Believe
It can
Achieve
—Napoleon Hill, author: Think and Grow Rich (1883-1970)

It takes as much courage to have tried and failed as it does to have tried and succeeded.
—Anne Morrow Lindbergh, author (1906-2001)

Liberty means responsibility. That is why most men dread it.
—George Bernard Shaw, 1925 Nobel Prize Winner in Literature (1856-1950)

Don't go around saying the world owes you a living. The world owes you nothing. It was here first.
—Mark Twain, author (1835-1910)

No one can possibly achieve any real and lasting success or "get rich" in business by being a conformist.
—J. Paul Getty, businessman (1892-1976)

⮂ Secret 10 ⮀
Careful Planning
This Is Really The Greatest Secret Of All!!!

Most people spend more time planning their vacations and evenings out, than they do planning their family finances! Think about it, vacations are usually very well and very carefully planned.

We take into consideration all kinds of things like: When will we leave? What do we need to do before we go? What will we bring along? How will we get to the airport? What will we do when we get there? How will we get to the hotel and around town? Where will we eat? And so on.

Are you that detailed with your personal finances? Be really honest with yourself. Do you really take the time to plan for your own future in such thorough detail? Probably not. It takes a lot of time, and knowledge, to analyze and plan your money.

I understand. I know that raising a family can be as much a full time job as "work" itself. There is seldom little time left to study tax laws and other financial information. Therefore, the job of planning your finances is often delayed until a "more convenient" time.

And, I also know that this secret may not sound as interesting as the others, because it requires more mundane tasks but it is...

121

The Key To Beating Revenue Canada, And Anyone Else Who Is After Your Money!

As a matter of fact, those who have taken the time to plan are more likely to have more money than those who don't plan. Especially when it comes to taxes. Planning regularly, and often, is your best weapon, to keep the taxman's greedy hands out of your pocket. It really is!

The message is getting through. "All taxed out, Canadians are turning to tax avoidance in record numbers. Half of Canadian taxpayers say they are now actively trying to cut the amount of taxes they pay each year." COMPAS poll: Nov 1997.

If you feel like the government has control over you; that can be fixed very quickly. But, the initial step must be yours. Taking that first step into a new life of lower taxes is really all up to you. All it takes is careful financial planning.

People sometimes have concerns about the financial planning process. The reason for this is that the process is unknown to them, and we are naturally afraid of the unknown. But, the people, who truly succeed financially, have learned to break out of their comfort zone. They have learned the right questions to ask and where to find the answers. I will try to demystify the financial planing process by answering the most frequently asked questions about financial planning. The following are a few of the most important questions people have asked me about financial planning:

What Are The Benefits Of A Financial Plan?

Simply put, a financial plan is designed to benefit you by providing you with alternatives, strategies, concepts, and well-thought out recommendations for all aspects of your financial life.

What Is The Financial Planning Process?

1. First, your financial planner must find out how you feel about your money and finances. Identifying and establishing your specific goals and objectives.

2. Then, the planner must get a detailed understanding of your income, assets, debts, company benefits, etc. Collecting and analyzing all relevant information on your financial situation.

3. And finally, the planner will draw up an action plan that addresses all your concerns and gives you choices. Then, and only then, will you be able to choose for yourself which way to go.

This process allows you the opportunity to make decisions from an educated position. There is nothing wrong with buying financial products from your financial planner, as long as they fit your needs and help you achieve your goals and objectives. However, buying financial products without a plan is like having surgery without an examination. I would never let a doctor operate on me without a complete diagnosis. Likewise, you should never let a financial planner sell you any financial products without an analysis and a plan.

A financial plan may be many things. It can be as short as one page or as thick as a set of tables, charts, and graphs. One is not necessarily better than the other. It just depends on how detailed your needs are. But, even if the written plan is short, the interview process must not be.

How Do You Select A Financial Planner?

There are many good financial planners who can truly help you accomplish your goals and objectives. But, just like in every other industry, there are financial planners who might hinder, rather than advance your financial progress. To separate the best from the rest, ask them questions. Here's a list of questions a prospective financial planner should be able to answer to your satisfaction:

1. **Ask for references.** The planner should be able to provide references from clients and other professionals. A planner may be able to produce client references but if they cannot produce references from other professionals, that might mean he or she is not respected by his or her peers.

2. **Ask the planner to outline the process he or she goes through to arrive at recommendations.** What you want to hear is an answer similar to the one I've written above, answering the question, "What is the financial planning process?"

3. **Ask how the planner is expecting to get paid.** No one works for free! They either charge fees, earn commission from selling financial products, or both. There is nothing wrong with the planner earning income from any of these, only that you should know how they get

paid. If the planner earns 100% of his or her income from commission then they must sell enough to earn a living and make up for the people who don't buy. If a fee is charged, do not pay more than 50% of the fee in advance. Although a retainer is often requested, most professionals do not require 100% or their fee in advance.

4. **Ask the planner about their experience and qualifications.** You've probably heard the expression: Some people have 10 years of experience, while others have 1 year of experience 10 times over. But, as a rule of thumb, if you have significant wealth, consider working with a financial planner who has at least 5 plus years of experience. Although there might be many good planners with less experience, why take the chance. It only makes sense to select a financial planner who has more experience than you.

5. **Ask how the planner keeps current.** With the constant changes and the barrage of new information, how do they keep up. Do they rely on information from a parent company? Do they go to seminars? Do they attend conferences? What do they read and do they subscribe to financial publications? If so, which ones? Are they studying for an advanced degree or designation? It is impossible for anyone to be an excellent financial planner unless they continually update themselves with current and accurate information!

6. **Ask the planner what outside professionals they bring into cases.** When or for what reason do they bring them in? No one can be the expert on everything. If your

planner is not an expert on your particular situation, you either need to find one that is or insist that he or she bring in an outside professional to help.

7. **Ask to see the financial strength of the companies the planner recommends.**

8. **Ask for a satisfaction guarantee.** The benefit you receive must be greater than the planning fees you have to pay.

What Do All The Designations Mean?

There is an alphabet soup of designations and sponsoring or professional associations, how can you tell them apart and what do they all mean? This is not meant as an endorsement of any designation, only as an explanation of what they mean and how a planner comes by wearing one.

Certified Financial Planner **CFP** — The CFP designation is given to financial planners who have successfully completed extensive studies in the area of financial planning. To qualify, a financial planner must successfully complete an education program and meet annual license requirements of the Financial Planners Standards Council.

Registered Financial Planner **RFP** — The Canadian Association of Financial Planners grants this designation. It is given to those who have extensive financial planning experience and who pass a comprehensive 6-hour exam.

Chartered Life Underwriter **CLU** — The Canadian Association of Insurance and Financial Advisors grants the CLU designation. A CLU is an established life insurance professional with a solid track record. He or she is qualified to deal in most fields of life and health insurance.

Chartered Financial Consultant **Ch.F.C.** — The Canadian Association of Insurance and Financial Advisors grant this designation. It is an advanced 3-course program, which follows the 12-course program of CLU.

Here are the web addresses to the professional financial planning organizations that oversee, provide education, and write standards for financial planners in Canada. On these websites you'll find additional useful information on financial planning:

Financial Planners Standards Council
www.cfp-ca.org

Canadian Association of Insurance and Financial Advisors
www.caifa.com

Canadian Association of Financial Planners
www.cafp.org

In conclusion I hope I have educated you, entertained you, and motivated you to do something to gain back control. If I have, that's great! Then I've accomplished what I set out to do. Now it's time to do your part while this is fresh on your mind, and you are still excited about the possibilities!

I encourage you to **start the planning process today.**

By the way, I hear all the time, "I already have an accountant, why do I need a financial planner?" I say, "That's good I have an accountant too!" But, you see their job is to record history. To tell you what you did in the past. They do an excellent job of that. But, when it comes to creative tax planning, most of them are either not geared up to handle the job or they're too busy to be looking into the future.

Canadians consult a wide variety of sources for tax planning advice. Family, friends, and accountants are no longer the main or only sources of information. Financial planners (54%) and professional tax planners (49%) are quickly catching up to family and friends (58%) and accountants (59%) as Canadians' chief counselors on cutting taxes. Source: The Financial Post/COMPAS poll conducted October 1997.

The Last Word

You must take the time to plan your taxes, so that they don't plan you! Learn these secrets, and feel the joy of knowing you are paying the least amount possible, with the safety of the law backing you up. Remember that our politicians make this stuff up, and it is your duty as a Canadian to follow and use the laws they make for us! You wouldn't want to disappoint them, would you?

**Plan Today...
Top of the World
Tomorrow!**

Useful Websites

David M. Voth
www.davidvoth.com

The Fraser Institute
www.fraserinstitute.ca

CATO Institute — Research and Liberty Information
www.cato.org

COMPAS — Research and Surveys
www.compas.ca

Revenue Canada — Canada Customs and Revenue Agency
www.ccra-adrc.gc.ca

The Supreme Court of Canada
www.scc-csc.gc.ca

Statistics Canada
www.statcan.ca

Canadian Taxpayer Federation
www.taxpayer.com

Canadian Tax Foundation
www.ctf.ca

CanadaInfo.net — Popular website for information
on Canada
www.canadianinfo.net

Bankers Almanac — Information on world banks and
their ranking
www.bankersalmanac.com

Reference Desk — Best source for facts on the Internet
www.refdesk.com

International Society for Individual Liberty (ISIL)
www.isil.org

The Future of Freedom Foundation
www.fff.org

BuildFreedom.com — Practical freedom information and
links to hundreds of sites
www.buildfreedom.com

Laissez Faire Books — The world's best selection of books
on Liberty
www.laissezfairebooks.com

> *Is life so dear, or peace so sweet, as to be purchased at the price of chains and slavery? Forbid it, Almighty God! I know not what course others may take, but as for me, give me liberty or give me death!*
> —Patrick Henry, patriot, orator, and statesman (1736-1799)

Notes

Notes

Notes

Notes

Order Form

Who do you know that would like to keep the tax-man's hands out of their pocket? Everyone can benefit from reading **The 10 Secrets Revenue Canada Doesn't Want You To Know!** - It's a perfect gift!

Please rush me _____ copies of **The 10 Secrets Revenue Canada Doesn't Want You To Know!** at $16.95 plus $3.00 Shipping and Handling plus GST ($21.35 total per copy).

Fax orders to: 306-934-0484

❑ Bill my Credit Card:　❑ VISA　❑ MASTERCARD
Card Number: _____
Expiry Date: _____

Name: _____
Address: _____
City: _____ Province: _____
Postal Code: _____ Phone: (_____) _____
E-mail: _____
Signature: _____

For any order of 10 or more books, please contact us by fax, phone or E-mail regarding our discount pricing.

Liberty House Publishing
Fax: (306) 934-0484　Phone: (306) 955-3838
E-mail: libertyhouse@shaw.ca